Reference Service and Sources

Dr. C.K. Sharma

ATLANTIC®
PUBLISHERS & DISTRIBUTORS

Published by
ATLANTIC®
PUBLISHERS & DISTRIBUTORS
B-2, Vishal Enclave, Opp. Rajouri Garden,
New Delhi-110027
Phones : 25413460, 25429987, 25466842

Sales Office
7/22, Ansari Road, Darya Ganj,
New Delhi-110002
Phones : 23273880, 23275880, 23280451
Fax : 91-11-23285873
web : www.atlanticbooks.com
e-mail : info@atlanticbooks.com

Printed in India
at Nice Printing Press, Delhi

Preface

Reference Service and Sources are not a modern concept but a continuing process of searching the reading material and sharpening the studies and researches. The importance of reference services cannot be overemphasised. It is a matter of fact that man thinks, works and acts to achieve some or the other objectives for which he needs to learn more and more. Accordingly, the requirement of study material keeps on growing.

Library is a centre of learning and the reference sources are the foundation of knowledge. Each library provides the readers with up-to-date information through its huge collection of books as well as reference sources like dictionaries, atlases, encyclopaedias and guides. The help, contact and liberal services providing explanation and assistance to the readers in their reading and research through reading material is called Reference service. Such services enable the readers to utilize the collection to the maximum.

Despite its usefulness, there are few books on Reference service and sources. Realising this scarcity, I have attempted to bring out a complete book on Reference and I am hopeful that it will prove immensely useful to teachers, research scholars and students of all levels. Knowledge of reference services and sources will also be useful for common man in their use of libraries. Incidentally, this is my thirty first book in the filed of library science and I am optimistic that like my other books, the present book will also receive overwhelming response from the readers.

I would like to take this opportunity to thank all my friends and colleagues who have always helped and encouraged me in my literary pursuits. I admire my both grandsons-in-law, Sonu and Monu, who inspired me to write the present book.

I convey my sincere thanks to Dr. K.R. Gupta, Chairman, M/s Atlantic Publishers and Distributors, New Delhi for excellent production and speedily completing the job.

C.K. SHARMA

Contents

PART – II
REFERENCE SOURCES

PART – I
REFERENCE SERVICE

Introduction

1

(A) REFERENCE SERVICE

Library has been an important institution since long ago in the society. Manuscripts were preserved in libraries in ancient time. These were preserved under some persons or institutions like temples, vihars, churches etc. The collections were allowed for consultation by the special persons or the members of the Royal families. Common man was not allowed to enter the premises of such collection. Librarians were called caretakers and their duty was to protect the collection. Libraries in ancient period were small and sometimes a part of religious place. Knowledge was limited. Collection was limited. Samuel Ratistin says that the total collection of all American libraries was 10 lakhs in 1850. Librarians were not providing reference service in 18th century.

After 1850 there was an effort to prepare a plan for the development of libraries. The Governments of England and United States promulgated library act in their countries. This resulted in increasing the number of readers and collection. Readers started demanding more and more books and also information which they required in their studies. The first effort was made in 1876 when libraries sought to help the readers in their need of information. This was the suggestion of Samuel Swetgreen who invited librarians and organized a conference in Philadelphia. Many papers were presented in the conference including an important paper "Personal Relations between Librarians and Readers", presented by Samuel Swetgreen. He stressed on good relations among librarians and readers which could provide a clear concept of library working and activities. He pointed out two reasons for developing such relations: (i) Personal relations; (2) Regular service regarding collection. Both the factors facilitated the readers' service and led to the emergence of reference service.

In 1877, a conference was held in which England and United States coordinated and the librarians of both the countries participated and discussed problems related to readers service. Melvil Dewey called this conference a step further regarding readers' satisfaction. It was also felt that Reference Service is a must to every library. In 1896 American Library Association adopted the Reference service as its regular service. Thus the concept that trained librarians are of much more importance in this regard has been established. Trained librarians can efficiently serve the readers and may provide better reference service.

In 1981 Education Act was passed by the House of Common, England in which a plan regarding literary expansion and education extension was approved and this Act also emphasised the need for library development. It was also felt that reference service can help in the educational development of the country.

It resulted in a general discussion in various conferences and seminars. Melvil Dewey expressed his views in one of the conferences:

> Librarian is not limited to the care, protection and collection of the reading material, but to provide necessary material to the students and teachers on their demand for their maximum satisfaction.

(B) DEVELOPMENT OF REFERENCE SERVICE

Reference Service was first started in United States and a specific preferential service in libraries was provided under it. It was adopted by many libraries or say majority of libraries including national libraries, state libraries, university and college libraries and other libraries. Librarians offered personal and cooperative services and also helped the readers through telephone and postal facilities. It was thought the main and moral duty of the librarian to provide all necessary help to readers. Trained and professional librarians were appointed in all libraries. Reference service was declared as one of the important parts of library services. Every library establishes a separate Reference Department as its one unit and a reference librarian is appointed for the smooth functioning of the department. Its staff other than the Reference Librarian have specialization in reference service.

Before planning the development of the reference service, the following points are to be taken into account:

1. How much facilities are to be provided?
2. What type of readers are to be served?
3. What are the sources required to serve the readers?
4. How to help the newcomers who enter the library?

There are researches being conducted in every field of discipline, which is creating new literature in various languages. It has become very difficult to search the required information out of the huge literature and collection. Therefore, it is very necessary for the libraries to serve the researchers with their required informations without any delay. Reference service serves this objective with the help of reference sources, *i.e.* Bibliographies, Indexes, Abstracts, translations, etc. It is the duty of the Reference librarian to make the readers aware about the latest informations received in the library from time to time.

(C) REFERENCE SERVICE IN INDIA

Dr. S.R. Ranganathan realized the importance of Reference librarian while he was on visit to London. He decided that such services should be introduced in Indian libraries to enable the readers to get their information. Dr. Ranganathan started Reference service in Madras University in 1926. In 1930, Ranganathan enunciated fundamentals and principles called "Five Laws of Library Service" which directed the libraries to function effectively in the socialistic pattern of society.

The main objective of the libraries is to spread the library among the people of the society and save the time of the readers. Reference service helps to fulfil this objective. Dr. Ranganathan established a separate department 'Reference

Department' in Madras University Library. He appointed 5 reference librarians. He gave them necessary training for reference services for a period of 3 months or short term training in Madras University Library.

There are following factors involved in need of Reference service:

(a) There should be a separate Reference Department.

(b) A Reference librarian should be the In-charge of the Department.

(c) Readers should be aware with the importance of the Reference Department.

(d) There should be a good collection of Reference sources.

(e) Collection should be according to the needs of the readers.

(f) Trained staff should be appointed in this department.

(g) Sufficient budget should be allotted to Reference Department.

(h) Reference Department should have Reprography facilities and Documentation work as its unit.

University Grants Commission and other funding departments of the Government are providing sufficient grant to the large libraries to develop their infrastructure which resulted an effective reference service. In this way Reference service has got an important place in Indian libraries.

(D) WHAT IS REFERENCE SERVICE

Library is a centre of learning. It organises the literature of various fields and interests and provides it to the readers its maximum use. Libraries are the backbone of the society as they provide a variety of informations to variety of readers with the help of trained and efficient library staff. A library with huge collection has no value, like a store in a grain field until unless the collection is widely used and benefited by the users or readers. It should save the time of the readers to utilize the collection to the maximum. It was felt to start such library service which could provide up-to-date and pinpointed service to the readers by providing them the required information in time. It is possible by reference service, in which library provides necessary information to the readers through personal contact, relations with the help of books and non-book material, received from time to time in the library. This service is called Reference service. Dr. Ranganathan has given top priority to this service. There are a few works which make the reference service more effective and sharp, *i.e.* Book selection, acquisition, classification and cataloguing, etc.

Some of the famous librarians have defined the reference service as under:

J.E. Waire – "The help, contact and liberal services providing explanation and help to the readers in their reading and research through reading material is called Reference service."

Margret Hutchins – "Reference work includes the direct personal aid within a library to person in search of information."

A.B. Kroeger – "Assistance in the use of resources of the library."

William Warner Bishop – "Reference work in an organized effort on the part of the libraries in aid of the most expeditious and fruitful use of their libraries."

A.L.A. Glossary of library terms – "That phase of library work which is directly concerned with assistance to readers in securing information and in using the resources of the library in study and research."

Louis Shores – "Reference is to library service what intelligence is to the military."

Pieres Butler – "It is the process by which civilized man is able to obtain specific information at will by the use of the books which have been organized into a library."

S.R. Ranganathan – "Reference service is establishing the contact between reader and book by personal service."

After studying the above definitions, it is clear that the help given to the readers in his information receipt through personal contact and relation is a Reference service. There are minor differences of opinion in definitions of the library professionals. Some interpret that the reference service is related to collection and its informations while modern library professionals are of opinion that Reference service is not limited to a library but it a co-operational effort of the libraries to answer the queries of the readers. If the information is not available in a library, it may take help of the other library through various resources. Therefore, Reference service is a human service which provides all necessary informations to the readers by any means of cooperation and coordination among libraries.

In nutshell we can say – Reference service is a personal service which aims to provide information to the reader who requires it. This service is:

(a) to answer the queries of the readers;

(b) to provide personal guidance how to consult the reference sources;

(c) to encourage the maximum use of the library collection.

(E) NEED OF REFERENCE SERVICE

It is evident that Reference service is no doubt a must service in libraries. With the advent of Printing Press the collection increased in various forms. Readers were very few. Librarian is always supposed to know about the collection of the library. Reader also knows something or the reference of the reading material. In such case there is hardly any need of librarian's help to the readers. But if reader is not aware with the new arrivals and other material or its contents, he needs the help of the Reference librarian. Moreover there is continuous growth of documents and it is very difficult for the reader to know the new documents and hence requires the help of the librarian for informations. There is knowledge explosion and it is very difficult to search the required information out of the millions of documents. Librarian organizes and controls the vast knowledge and presents it before the readers. It is just to trace the pearl in an ocean.

Dr. S.R. Ranganathan stressed the following points to provide reference service.

(1) Artificiality of Books

In modern time there is a large production of reading material and it is a continuing process. It is very difficult to organize the literature and understand the whole, by the reader. It is a tedious job. It involves huge funds and labour. Hence, it is necessary to understand the collection and provide reference service to the readers.

(2) Complexity of Catalogue

Different libraries follow different catalogue code to prepare catalogue cards or cataloguing. Catalogue cards are arranged differently according to the nature of the code. Though library catalogue is prepared and used for providing necessary information regarding collection of the library, it is necessary to provide information to the newcomers about the library collection, which is possible by personal contact or reference service.

According to Dr. S.R. Ranganathan "Book selection, book order, periodical works, classification, cataloguing, accessioning, organization and display of books and charging and discharging will become fruitless unless proper reference service is done." Indeed, reference service alone can lead to the ultimate fulfilment of the service of a library and of the 'Five Laws of Library Science'.

There are many reasons for the need of effective reference service:

1. To save the time of the readers.
2. To present the existing literature containing new information.
3. To decentralization of new informations.
4. To modernise the new equipment and systems.
5. To implement five laws of library science.
6. To be aware of the various methods of the library.
7. To make the complexity understand classification and cataloguing.

Therefore, the difficulties come in the way and to remove them, to save time of the readers to make them aware of the library systems and to fulfil the objects of the library, reference service is the only tool.

(F) PURPOSE OF REFERENCE SERVICE

Following are the main objectives of reference service:

1. To protect and arrange the collection.
2. To present the collection before the readers.
3. To have trained and professional librarian.
4. To encourage coordination between employees and readers.
5. To save the time of the reader.
6. To conduct fact-finding research.
7. To develop the library.
8. To maximise use of reference services.

(1) Protection and Arrangement of Books

In fact the work of protection and presentation/conservation of collection is not the work of Reference librarian or Reference department. It was in ancient time when the protection was the main work of the librarian, caretaker or archivists. But now the main aim is to arrange them and put them for their maximum use for their users. There are many precautions taken to protect them. Every precaution is taken while constructing a building, providing furniture, and arranging the collection. There are many modern techniques also. Reference librarian takes all such precautions also. He arranges and protects the reference sources while serving the readers so that an effective reference service may be provided.

(2) Presenting the Collection

Reference service makes the whole collection usable. Every reading material is used in one time or the other. There are readers for every document and Reference librarian makes it possible. Libraries have changed in its form and shape. Old concept has gone. Modern libraries are adopting all activities and methods by which every document can be put on service to the readers. New and valuable books are purchased, accessioned and properly arranged on the shelf so that they may be easily approachable. Libraries are preparing bibliographies and indexes to help the reader to search his book. Dr. S.R. Ranganathan, when visited America, he asked the librarian of a college of USA "How many books are used out of your collection". The answer was "only two" which still could attract the attention of the readers. Thus, reference library makes all efforts for the maximum use of the documents.

(3) Need for Trained Librarian

Reference service and trained librarian both supplement each other. Both can be successful with cooperation of each other. Trained librarian is fully aware of library techniques and fully efficient to provide reference service. Reference sources help him in selecting the best and useful books. Reference librarian cannot provide efficient and adequate service without proper reference sources. Modern techniques including automation equipments also help the Reference librarian to serve exhaustively and quickly. Reference service increases the number of trained librarians who are always proved a boon to the researches and national development.

(4) Cooperation between Readers and the Staff

Reference service develops relations among readers and library staff. Every increase and extension of reference service will need more staff to serve the readers. Hence, there is a great need of cooperation among readers and the staff. Their cooperation will be useful because:

(a) It will develop the library service.

(b) It will attract the readers towards library collection.

(c) Readers will put up their problems.

(d) Staff and readers will solve their problems with personal contact.

(e) Staff help in researches and higher studies.

J.H. Shera has explained in his book 'social foundation of librarianship' that library development can be achieved by effective reference service. Books are never useless. Every book has a reader but reader should be aware about the book. Books are always useful as they entertain the readers, change their nature and develop their knowledge and energy. All this is possible by good personal relations among the staff and the readers.

(5) Saves the Time of the Reader

Every reader wants to receive his information immediately. It is possible by reference service only. Reference service should be such which could help the reader to solve his problems and provide necessary information in response to queries of the readers. Reader should be given maximum facilities as to seek information in minimum time. Reference service saves the time of the reader. Indian libraries do not provide necessary facilities, do not have trained Reference librarians. But in Metropolitan cities and in large libraries effective reference service is being provided.

There are many reasons that libraries are facing problems in providing effective reference service, such as:

(a) Paucity of funds.

(b) Lack of manpower.

(c) Lack of trained librarians

(d) Lack of proper collection.

(e) Lack of library facilities.

(f) Lack of cooperation and coordination.

All above reasons could not adopt the modern techniques in most of the libraries in India. Reader spends his most of the time in searching the document and information. Reference librarian can solve all these problems and can save the time of the readers.

(6) Fact-finding Research

Reference service encourages researches. Researchers generally spend their maximum time in searching informations. They are not aware of the library techniques and systems. It is the duty of Reference librarian to make the researchers aware of the new arrivals and reference sources which could help them to conduct his research efficiently.

(7) Library Development

Reference service is first step in the development of libraries. An effective and adequate reference service increases the number of readers which helps in the smooth running of all other departments. It requires a proper staff and adequate place for the reference service. It leads the library towards modernization. Reference service has caused space problem as it has increased a good number of staff and readers.

(8) Use of Reference Sources

There are most of the reference sources which are costly and need regular attention for their use. Any misuse or unusable position can effect the library development. Reference service speeds up the development. Reference librarian provides training to the readers and laymen, newcomers to the library and it encourages the reading habits among the readers. In spite of this, Reference department provides reading material housed in other libraries also.

Thus, Reference service encourages the readers for the maximum use of the library, maximum use of library collection, saves the time of the reader, satisfying five laws of library science. Therefore, it popularizes the library and contributes to the national development.

(G) FUNCTIONS OF REFERENCE SERVICE

Reference service has a wider area. It is very difficult to calculate its activities. American Library Association has enumerated following functions:

(1) Supervisory functions
(2) Instructional functions
(3) Informatory functions
(4) Guidance functions
(5) Appraisal functions
(6) Bibliographical functions.

(1) Supervisory Functions

It is the main function of Reference librarian. Supervisory functions include:

(a) Organization of reference department
(b) Guidance to the staff of reference department
(c) Management of reference sources
(d) Other preparatory functions.

(2) Instructional Functions

Instructional functions include:

(a) Use of reference sources.
(b) Guidance for the use of reference sources.
(c) Guidance to readers to search the required book independently.
(d) Make the readers awarè of:
   (i) All departments
   (ii) Library catalogue
   (iii) Classification
   (iv) Self arrangement
   (v) Collection of the library
   (vi) Reference sources.

(3) Informatory Functions

Reader generally enters the library for some informations. He wants to consult the books and journals for which he needs guidance about the related department, its functions, working, collection and is likely to search or enquire about a particular book, *e.g.* Autobiography of Mahatma Gandhi or the name of the books to which Nobel Award's are given. There are many readers who need such informations which are available in the documents kept in other libraries. Such informations take time to answer and reply. This is possible by reference service only. Informations are provided through telephone also.

(4) Guidance Function

Reference service involves guidance. Reader is given guidance regarding:

(a) Use of library

(b) Use of books

(c) Self-consultation

(d) Function of the library

(e) Duties of library staff

(f) Function of the various departments.

Reference librarian's responsibility is to provide necessary guidance for the maximum use of the library and collection.

(5) Bibliographical Function

Reference department prepares bibliographies for the easy search of the documents. Reference librarian is always in contact with researchers and other readers and makes them aware of latest literature and provides bibliography if required by the readers. Bibliographical services are very important and helpful to the researchers also.

(6) Appraisal Functions

Reference librarian conducts evaluation programme of the effectiveness and quality of the:

(a) Reference work

(b) Reference services

(c) Reference staff

An appraisal is applied to know the use of the collection and the service. Reference librarian and reference staff should evaluate their own services also. There are a few scales to evaluate the effectiveness of the reference service, such as:

(a) Whether the query of the reader is properly analysed?

(b) Whether proper procedure or process is followed?

(c) Whether the reader is provided information with full satisfaction?

(d) Whether library has sufficient reference sources?

If all above questions are satisfactorily answered, it is assumed that service is effective and efficient.

Prof. A.K. Mukharjee has mentioned the following functions of the reference service:

(a) Prompt answer of the queries of the readers personally or by phone or post.

(b) Provide help to the readers for the maximum use of the library resources.

(c) Make available all necessary informations to readers.

(d) Prepare bibliographies or profiles.

(e) Prepare indexes and abstracts and make them available to the readers for their use.

(f) Provide photocopy of the micro-thoughts.

(g) Provide inter-library loan service.

(h) Preserve rare collection for its use.

(i) Provide translation service.

(j) Seek cooperation from documentation and information centres.

(k) Collect important informations relating to the collection of libraries at regional and international level.

(l) Provide microfilm of the important documents.

(m) Provide necessary informations to research scholars, scientists and technicians.

(n) Retrieve informations pertaining to research.

Kinds of Reference Service 2

There are two kinds of reference services:

(A) Ready Reference Service

(B) Long Range Reference Service

(A) READY REFERENCE SERVICE

Reference service is a process in which readers receive their information through personal contact of the Reference librarian. There are queries of many types, varieties, and are time bound. Reference department always make efforts to remove the difficulties of the readers to fulfil their requirements.

Therefore, all such information which are provided to readers immediately are called Ready reference service. American Library Association called it "Direct Reference Service." Dr. S.R. Ranganathan has defined it as "Ready Reference Service is reference service finished or replied in a very short time in a minute if possible." Therefore, Ready reference service is important reference service and it is related to such informations which are provided directly by the Reference librarian and that too in short period. It also includes such reference services which direct the readers to reference sources immediately and information is gathered within short time.

Ready reference service includes the following queries:

(a) Which are demanded direct.

(b) Which are demanded by sharp medias.

(c) Which are simple.

(d) Which are answered on the table of Reference librarian.

(e) Which involves short answers.

(f) Which are responded within short time or within 5 minutes or less.

Examples — Queries

1. How many states are in Indian territory?
2. Literary percentage of Andhra Pradesh?
3. Address of Lucknow University?
4. Library Education Centres in India?

All such answers can be given within short time. Reference librarian either refers the names of reference sources or answers the query immediately.

Reference sources: Ready Reference queries are always 'Fact-finding queries'. Louis in his book 'Basic Reference Service' has given such reference sources which are helpful in giving reply of queries within short time. Important references sources are:

(a) Dictionary
(b) Directories / Hand books
(c) Census reports
(d) Year books / Annuals
(e) Biographies
(f) Gazetteer
(g) Atlas
(h) Encyclopedias, etc.

(a) Need of Ready Reference Service

It is seen that readers have knowledge of books which are generally concerned with their studies. But sometimes the reader needs such informations which are not known to them and their queries are also not related to their concerned books. Reference books are such books which are referred and consulted as and when any information is needed. Therefore, readers are not aware of reference books. Moreover, reference service sources are also arranged differently which is also not properly known to the readers.

Thus, reference service is an essential service to all readers who come to library for their studies.

(b) Procedure

Ready Reference service is basically completed in three phases. All these three phases are interrelated to and sometimes used together. They are:

(a) Preparation

(b) Service

(c) Assimilation

Preparation

In this stage librarian prepares himself by:

(1) Keeping knowledge about the department and its activities:

(i) having knowledge of reference sources.

(ii) maintaining the reference counter and reference diary.

(iii) maintaining himself with current knowledge.

(2) Organizing the Reference department:

(i) by maintaining the reference department.

(ii) by arranging the reference sources systematically.

(iii) knowledge of publication of new reference sources and the latest editions of reference sources.

(3) Arranging the literature which has not been organized but is very useful for ready reference service.

(c) Service

After preparation, reference service is provided. Service is given as under:

(i) Analysing the reader's query.

(ii) Determining the reference source pertaining to some information.

(iii) Informing the reader about reference source.

(iv) Guide the reader how to consult the reference source, so that reader may himself consult the reference source independently.

(d) Assimilation

It is related with following things:

(a) Recording of information received.

(b) Sharing the views and efforts made in tracing the informations.

(c) Reference service is not complete by receiving the information but it should be kept in mind that this information may be used by other readers also.

(d) One information may be developed by more than one reader. Hence, information should always be living/ ready and recorded.

(e) As much as Reference librarian gains experience in providing reference service, it should be discussed with other staff members.

(B) LONG RANGE REFERENCE SERVICE

Long range reference service indicates long time in providing reference service. This service is given:

1. To special readers demanding special informations.
2. Normally in long time, *i.e.* more than 5 minutes.
3. With the help of reference sources.
4. More in special libraries than other libraries.

Dr. S.R. Ranganathan stressed that Long Range Reference Service is more used in public and special libraries. It is not practised in every library. School libraries have no reference service but it is much more needed in technical and industrial libraries.

Long range reference service involve:

(a) Much time

(b) Normal guidance

(c) For research scholars, scientists or special readers

(d) In higher education.

(a) Short Range and Long Range Reference Service — A Difference

Dr. S.R. Ranganathan has given 3 points of difference between short range reference service and long range reference service.

(i) *Time involved*

Long range reference service involves much time while short range reference service takes very short time. Short range reference service is provided immediately or within very short period. It answers the query quickly and takes one minute to 5 minutes. But it takes much more time to answer the queries in long range reference service. It may take sometimes even more than half an hour.

Sometimes long range reference service turns to short range reference service. When a long reference service has been provided and the result of the queries is recorded at reference desk, next time it will become short range reference service and will take short time to answer the queries.

(ii) *Material used*

There are different reference sources used for long range reference service and short range reference service. Short range reference queries need reference sources like Dictionary, year-book, handbook and encyclopedia, etc. while long range reference queries need information sources like bibliographies, indexes, abstracts, and bibliography of bibliographies. These reference sources may direct the reader to trace his information. Periodicals and pamphlets are also helpful in long range reference service. Even if any source does not satisfy the reader, other libraries in the country or out of country may be consulted for the purpose of providing information.

(iii) *Information sought*

All queries covered by short range reference service are:

(a) simple
(b) fact-finding
(c) short
(d) pinpointed
(e) involve short research process
(f) involve mostly single reference source
(g) readily available.

While in long range reference service queries are:

(a) complex
(b) detailed
(c) involve long research process
(d) involve more than one reference source.

(iv) ***Current information***

Such informations are fact-finding but such queries cannot be satisfied by short range reference service because reference sources cover such informations which happen before the publication of reference sources. Generally reference sources are published after a gap of one year, which is suitable for long range reference service. On the other hand all such informations which are fact-finding, are possibly available and served by short range reference service.

(v) ***Outdated information***

There are informations which are outdated and provided by long range reference service. Such informations are not current. For example Kargil war which was fought five years ago. What was its effect on economic conditions of India?

(vi) ***Complex informations***

There are a few informations which are complex and need consultation of more than 2 to 3 reference sources. Such informations are provided by long range reference service as it takes good time to consult and trace. Such informations are not dealt by short range reference service. For example: The role of libraries in activities of Adult education.

(vii) ***Information related to specialists***

Experts include research scholars, scientists and engineers. Such queries are related to specific informations. For examples, new inventions in the field of library classification, and new developments in cancer research. Such informations are gathered after consulting many sources and take a long time. Hence, such services are called long range reference service. Such queries are not covered in short range reference service.

(viii) ***Information related to a particular point of view***

There are informations which are available in foreign languages or in such language which is not known to the reader. Such informations come under the purview of long range reference service as it takes long time. Such informations are provided by translation service.

(ix) ***Information not available in the library***

There are few queries of such informations which are not available in the library. Such informations are gathered from other libraries or the experts.

(b) Need of Long Range Reference Service

There is a need of long range reference service at every step in a library. There are many reasons of it, some of which are discussed below:

(i) ***It saves the time of the readers and experts***

Time is precious for an expert and research scholars. They try to finish their research in minimum time to get the current result. But most of their time is spent in literature search. They search the literature to know the latest development in their respective fields. If librarian helps in literature search, it will save the time of the researchers and the experts. Librarian is aware about the reference sources and the procedures to search the required information.

(ii) ***Knowledge explosion***

20th century is a period of knowledge explosion. The literature is being produced in each subject field and it is very difficult to study the whole literature. Libraries build selected literature suited to the readers. Libraries purchase a good number of literature and reader is always eager to know the details and whereabouts of the literature received in library or published anywhere in the country or the world.

Reference librarian is well-versed and trained in the search techniques of literature. He can easily help the readers to trace his documents. Researchers and scientists waste their valuable time in searching the literature and knowing their whereabouts. They are also not aware of the development of their subject fields. Reference librarian always serves the reader with the help of reference tools like reference books, bibliographies, indexes, abstracts, directories, yearbooks, handbooks, etc.

(iii) *Complexity of information sources*

Information sources are many and full of complexities. Every information source has different arrangement, style of presentation, language barrier, which is not known to readers. Reference librarian with his abilities provides all informations to the readers.

(iv) *Information sources of other libraries*

No library is complete in itself. It is also not possible for a single library to house the whole literature published. Libraries take help of other libraries for using their information sources. Each library has limited funds. Information sources are in huge number which cannot be procured by one library. Therefore, libraries cooperate each other and utilize the information sources together. It is possible by resource sharing.

(c) Process of Long Range Reference Service

There are 3 steps of process:

(1) Preparation

(2) Service

(3) Assimilation

(1) Preparation

Librarian prepares himself with three devices to serve the readers:

(i) *Subject knowledge*

It is the first duty of the librarian to keep himself well-versed with the various subjects. For example a librarian is working in library of "Chemical Biology Institute" or "Institute of Economics", he should know about Chemical Biology or Economics. It does not mean that he should be a subject expert, but he should know the subject divisions, their special characteristics and various literature available on the subject. Only then he can answer the queries or guide the readers and provide Long Range Reference Service.

(ii) *Knowledge of information*

There are information sources in each subject of study. Librarian should have the knowledge of information sources, and their availability. He should also evaluate the reference sources which are more appropriate and useful. Important sources are indexes, abstracts, bibliographies. Librarian should manage and arrange the newspaper clipping to know the day-to-day affairs. There are other important sources like Research reports, Thesis and Biographies.

(2) Services

When librarian prepares himself with information sources, the following steps are to be taken to provide long range reference service.

(a) Selecting and Scrutinizing the Queries

There are questions which are multidimensional and complex. Such questions are to be studied, reviewed and their central theme or the problem should be determined. It is also necessary to know the depth of the question and the need of the reader. One question may have manyfold aspects. Whichever aspects a reader wants, should be known or studied by the librarian.

(b) Search of Information Sources

A librarian is always cautious about the readers' problems. He studies:

(i) Nature of the reader

(ii) Type of questions

(iii) Type of information sources required

(iv) The location where the source is available.

On the basis of the above stages, librarian searches for the source and makes it available to the readers or guides him to consult the same on the location it is available.

(c) Documentation

Documentation is an important source. Librarian prepares a list of books or non-book material which can guide the reader to receive information about his requirements.

Documentation lists are prepared on the demand of the reader. There are reference documents of other languages which are translated in favoured language and provided to the readers.

(3) Assimilation

Librarian reviews the long range reference services and sees the hindrances and difficulties which are to be redressed. In other words we may call it an evaluation of the long range reference service given by the librarian. He analyses his work and service. He also evaluates the reference sources as how much they are useful. Thus, the reference librarian arranges the informations subjectwise in view of the future demands. He also consults his colleagues and experts to uptodate the information sources.

(C) FIVE LAWS AND REFERENCE SERVICE

Dr. S.R. Ranganathan enunciated five laws of library science which cover the whole range and all aspects of library and information science. These five laws are the basis of a good library which is functional. Dr. Ranganathan gave a message to the librarians that if they want their libraries to be functional and service-oriented, they should follow five laws of library science. These laws have great importance in reference service. A successful reference service satisfies the five laws. Reference service is applied as tool/equipment of five laws of library science. Reference service establishes relations between librarian, reference sources and the readers. In other words reference service works as a chain between these three and helps in smooth running of the library.

Reference service satisfies the Five laws of library science in following ways:

(a) by personal contact;

(b) by understanding the queries of the readers;

(c) by making available the reference sources;

(d) by saving the time of the readers.

However, reference service develops the library activities.

First Law — Books / Documents are for use

Library is a centre of learning and hence maintains a collection of literature. Books are selected without any consideration of caste, creed and colour. Collection is not meant for storage or kept like warehouse, but it is put to active and regular use by the readers. Collection is never locked but presented or displayed before the readers. This work is more effectively made by the personal relations of Reference librarian. He attracts the readers and encourages them for the maximum use of the collection. He makes the readers aware about new collection received in the library from time to time. Reference library, if found necessary, arranges the Refresher course to let them know with the specialization of the library collection, various departments, and library facilities. They guide the readers to search the answer of their problems.

Readers have different nature, attitude, characteristics and demands. They enter the library with different problems and seek varied information. Some readers enter the library with no specific aim. Just they come to read something or simply to visit the library. Reference librarian stimulates them and attracts them to read the books of their choice. Reader likes the library with the sweet behaviour of the Reference librarian.

According to S. William — "Reference librarian establishes personal relations with the readers by his sweet behaviour, liberal attitude, knowledge and personality. In other words reference librarian is a friend, thinker and guide. Reference librarian should be a social person who believes in social welfare and social values. His aim should be to serve the society and cooperate in social activities. He should seek cooperation of library staff. In all, reference librarian's role should be to provide maximum service to the readers.

Second Law — Every reader and his book

It should be the objective of Reference librarian that every reader, whosoever he/she may be, should passess following qualities, which are considered to achieve this object:

(a) Reference librarian should be trained.

(b) All questions of a reader should be answered.

(c) Librarian and the senior library staff should be trained in Reference work and services.
(d) Reference librarian should have good knowledge of Reference sources.
(e) Reader should be aware and conscious about library reading and learning.

Reference librarian, if trained will understand the problems of the reader. He will study the reader's problems psychologically. If he is a learned person, he may have knowledge of books which will help him to provide library service in short time.

Bibliographies are important source of providing information of the reader. Other reference sources are dictionary, publishers catalogue, library catalogue. There are many publishers who publish bibliographies according to subjects, authors, titles, etc. All such bibliographies help the reader to search his book without wasting much time. Library catalogue also give necessary information about new arrivals of books and non-book material. Readers are being known about the catalogue because catalogue is being known about the library records. Catalogue is being used in schools also and students are well aware about the use of catalogue. Catalogue also fulfils the needs of readers in various directions by analyzing the subject of the book.

Second aspect of second law is reader. Readers should also shoulder their responsibilities to understand the library equipments, catalogue and other facilities provided by the library. They should follow library rules. They should borrow books for the number allotted to them and return them in time. This would help the library to serve other readers also. It will lead to maximum use of reading material.

Third Law — Every Book/Document and its reader

The following efforts are to be made to fulfil third law for every book/document and its reader:

(a) Open Access System
(b) Classification

(c) Cataloguing

(d) Display of new arrivals

(e) Special library services:

(1) Translation service

(2) Bibliographical/Documentation service

(3) Indexing service

(4) Organizing exhibition

(5) Book reviews

Open Access System is the first effort to implement open access system. Open access system means a free access of readers to the library to select and read the book of their choice. Reader should be free to move in all such department which provide reader's facilities. Readers should be assisted for his difficulties and he should not be pressed for reading the literature which is not of his choice.

Second effort is the use of simple, easy and convenient classification scheme which can be handled, and understood by any staff and the reader. Classification scheme should be such which can analyse the subject and arrange the subject in a systematic way. All books on specific subjects should be placed in its proper place, so that reader can approach the book independently. Library should have a catalogue based on standard code. Entries in card catalogue or in other modern form should be simple, sequential and systematic. A standard catalogue will help the reader to trace his book through author, title, subject, etc.

Reference librarian should attract the readers. He will help the reader to get his book. There are chances of decreasing human relations, but it is difficult to leave the reading habits if some one is habitual of reading. Therefore, it is the duty of the reference librarian to inculcate the reading habits in the readers. Librarian's behaviour, his ability, experience, systems, and liberal attitude attract the readers. Reference librarian keeps in personal contact with the readers and encourages them to use various resources of the library.

Book exhibitions should be organized to make the readers aware about new arrivals of documents. There are other efforts to be made, such as:

(1) Display of new arrivals on display board.

(2) Publishing the list of new arrivals in newspapers.

(3) Providing translation service.

(4) Preparing index, abstract, bibliographies on demand by the readers.

All these efforts keep the book in contact with the readers.

Fourth Law — Save the time of the reader

Reference service saves the time of the reader. Efficient and speedy reference service will help the reader to save his time. There are many components which could save the time of the reader:

(a) Well trained librarian

(b) Uptodate and adequate reference sources

(c) Reference service

(d) Classification

(e) Cataloguing

(f) Open access system

(g) Modern technology

There are two aspects of time saving:

(a) Short range reference service

(b) Long range reference service

(a) **Short range reference service**: The most important work is to initiate and welcome of newcomers in the library and guide them properly to satisfy their queries. Libraries establish Reference counter for this purpose which helps the readers to be aware with their demands of reading material and satisfies them with answers of such queries which may be answered within short span of time. Reference counter provides short range reference service. Reference counter is also known as 'Information desk' which provides information immediately. In Academic libraries students generally need new books of new editions. Reference librarian informs them about new arrivals concerning to their courses.

There are many types of readers, *e.g.* businessmen, officers, scientists, technicians who have less time and want immediate reply or availability of their required literature or information. They need information by telephone or other sources to get the answer of their queries. Reference librarian makes all informations available within no time. It saves the time of the reader and he need not walk in the library facing problem of where to trace his required information. Other departments and divisions also help the reader in manyfold problems, like:

(1) which literature is in need,

(2) which book is not available or already issued,

(3) when the book will be available.

(b) Long range reference service: There are queries of the reader which cannot be answered immediately by information desk or which require help of reference sources and are called long range reference sources. In long range reference service guidance and directions are considered very important. Such directions include guidance regarding library systems, use of reference sources, preparation of reference sources and their methods. Reference tools save the time of the readers. Readers search the answers of their queries with the help and guidance of the Reference librarian.

Fifth Law — Library is a growing organism

Library develops with the development of the reference service. Efficient and good reference service increases the number of the readers. With the growth in the number of the readers continues the growth of library collection, staff and the building. This will satisfy the fifth law.

In view of the above discussion of five laws of library science, it can be said that these laws will be satisfied if library collection is used to the maximum, every book is consulted by the reader, every reader finds/traces his book, time of the staff and the reader is saved and library develops in all its spheres.

Reference Librarian

3

Reference Librarian is supposed to have good relations with the readers and provide them with required reading material. Therefore, Reference Librarian is the person who can satisfy the readers and is also capable of satisfying his requirements. Moreover, it is he who can convince the readers to their maximum satisfaction. It is possible only if:

(a) Reader gets his information immediately,
(b) Reading facilities are conveniently available,
(c) Reader achieves his purpose for which he has entered the library,
(d) Reference Librarian applies his intelligence wisdom, ability, knowledge and experience to satisfy the reader,
(e) Reader is given answer to all his queries,
(f) Reading material is made available.

(A) QUALITIES OF A REFERENCE LIBRARIAN

A Reference Librarian is required to have following qualities:

(a) Library Training

Reference Librarian should be professionally trained. He should have a specialized training related to work, administration and organization. He should have a wide knowledge of reference sources, their uses and applications. In modern libraries modern techniques and appliances like computer and network are being used. Reference Librarian should have a good knowledge of computer, microfilming, etc. He should have up to date knowledge of new inventions and developments. There are many systems and techniques which may be applied for the better services of the reader. Reference

Librarian should be aware of the developments of all modern systems and techniques. To have good knowledge and understanding of all these things the Reference Librarian should undergo a training which will enable him to understand the difficulties of the reader and make necessary amendment in the systems on the basis of his experience. It will be economical and will add to the efficiency of the system.

Traditional Reference Librarian will not be successful in application of modern techniques and appliances. Reference Librarian should change himself with the changing scenario and adopt the modern systems and technologies in libraries. This is an age of information technology and a Reference Librarian should be well-equipped with the latest technical skills and expertise.

(b) Well Qualified

Reference Librarian should possess high academic qualifications. He should be an academician and possess the habits of reading and learning. He should have good understanding of new developments and apply them in the library. He should adjust himself with the circumstances and face them boldly.

(c) Patience

Sometimes when an experienced person who is working hard, becomes tired and looses his patience. But Reference Librarian never loses his patience. He always maintains his mental balance and controls his behaviour. According to Dr. S.R. Ranganathan, it is a normal quality of a Reference Librarian to maintain mental peace and patience. It is a saying that "once a professor enters the library and enquires about the details of Mira Bai after consulting all relevant books and puts up many questions before the Reference Librarian. The Reference Librarian faced all questions and made available all reading material pertaining to questions of the professor patiently and did not lose his temper and behaviour. Lastly, the professor was convinced and he felt sorry for his over the questioning and appreciated the Reference Librarian for his efficient handling of the situation.

It is very difficult for a Reference Librarian to have a good knowledge of all subjects. Every man has his individual liking or disliking, taste of reading and learning. He may have more knowledge in his own subject or the subject of his liking. If a person has achieved degree in economics, he will have more knowledge of economics in comparison to other subjects. Readers are of varied nature, choice knowledge and experience and have their individual varied queries. They need answer to their queries immediately. If they are not promptly provided with answers even they began to criticize the librarian and entire system. Sometimes readers even lose their temper. But Reference Librarian always responds with smile. Therefore, Reference Librarian should be jack of all trades.

(d) Psychological Behaviour

Readers are of different nature, behaviour and temperament. They have varied problems. Reference Librarian deals with readers of different caste, creed and colour, intelligence, etc. Reference Librarian deals with benefit to the clientele just like a trader. A trader is always polite with his customer and convinces him for his product and earns more profit. Similarly, a Reference Librarian attracts the readers with his polite behaviour. He psychologically studies the nature, behaviour and the learning taste of the readers and deals accordingly. Though it is a difficult task, but a Reference Librarian wins over it. He applies his intelligence and foresightness and provide library service. Moreover, Reference Librarian is like a dramatist and actor who plays an attracting drama and acts as per needs of the reader.

"For instance one student of B.A. enters the library and asks for a book on 'Introduction of Economics'. But due to non-availability of the book, librarian asks him to take another book on the same subject. He presents one book on 'Principles of Economics' and other book on 'Theory of Economics', but student could not be convinced. Librarian again showed him the contents of the book and convinced that these two books also covered his syllabus. At last student was convinced and took the book." This is the effort of the

Reference librarian who convinced the students by many angles and ultimately succeeded.

Therefore, Reference librarian studies the readers' choice and applies his psychological behaviour. He is always conscious about the psychology of the readers. He is always conscious about the needs of the researchers.

(e) Studious

Reference librarian should be an academician, learned man and a man of reading habits. He can solve many problems without any difficulty and without the help of Reference books. Books are of many varieties with different subjects but with different angles and points of view. It is very difficult for an author to express his views in depth on all aspects of a subject. Every author has specialization. Reference librarian provides necessary informations as per requirement of the readers problems, as he is fully aware of the fact-finding and specialized reference books. He knows the quality and demerits of the reference books. He has in his mind the difference of books, their subject matter and the thought contents of a author expressed in a book. Reference librarian never sits alone but always consults the books, reads them and notes down the special features of the books. He suggests the readers for more books to consult on the same problem. This way reader is benefited by the Reference librarian to the maximum.

(f) Sound Mind and Thinking

Reference librarian should have sound mind. Persons of temperaments, instable mind, are not supposed to be suitable reference librarians. Such persons are proved useless to the readers. They fail to attract the readers. Reference librarian with healthy mind provides reference service more efficiently.

Reference librarian should have free thinking. He presents fact-finding informations before the readers which is more beneficial to the readers. First Reference librarian hears the reader patiently, thinks over it, studies it and then answers the queries of the reader. Therefore, Reference librarian is supposed to know more about Reference books. He should not be prejudiced against any reader.

(g) Liberal Attitude, Sweet Voice, Good Personality and Sound Health

(1) **Liberal attitude:** Person with liberal attitude is always appreciated. Reference librarian should possess this quality. Liberal attitude always appreciate others and well-wisher of others.

(2) **Sweet voice:** Sweet voice always attracts a person. Reference librarian should have such sweet voice.

(3) **Good personality:** Good personality attracts others. People regard him. Reference librarian of good personality is also appreciated. Readers are generally satisfy with his answer if he is learned man with good personality.

(4) **Sound health:** Reference librarian should possess sound health. Readers always like a person who is not ill. A person of sound health will always be active and alert regarding his duties.

(h) Administrative Experience

Reference librarian should have an experience of administration and organization. He is supposed to be well-versed in all working and activities of all the departments of a librarian. Until and unless he is known with the functions of all departments, he cannot give proper directions to the reader. He may also shoulder responsibilities of other departments in addition to his own department. No doubt the working of Reference librarian is different from other librarians or department's incharge. But even then he should have knowledge of handling the equipments and technical know-how of these departments, *i.e.* technical work, cataloguing, bibliographic work, microfilming, and automation.

(B) DUTIES OF A REFERENCE LIBRARIAN

Dr. Ranganathan has proved on the basis of Vedas that reader is guest and an honourable man who is concerned with academic work. He is like a God to the library to whom the librarian should serve with zeal and jest. Reference librarian has following duties:

(a) Welcome the reader as he enters the library.

(b) Enquires with the reader, his problems and requirements.

(c) Answers the queries of the readers. Answer can be given through any media — Telephone, Telegraph, E-mail, Fax, etc. Personal questions may be answered immediately so that reader's time may be saved.

(d) Gives know-how about the specific features of the library and the Reference sources so that reader may search his document without others' help through cataloguing, classification, bibliographies, dictionary, encyclopedia, etc.

(e) Helps the reader in making the documents available through Inter-library loan at local, regional and national level.

(f) Provides translation service. Reference librarian should know more than two languages.

(g) Prepares bibliographies and make them available, *e.g.* Microfilm, Photostat facilities, computer facilities.

(h) Keepre in touch with documentation centre, Bibliographical centres, and help the reader.

(i) Provide information regarding documentation centers, information centers and keep in touch with them to provide necessary information to the readers.

Some Suggestions for Reference Librarian

Berry and Washerman has given following suggestions:

1. Many Reference librarians are not wise and they are more suitable to work in office. Such persons should not be given the responsibility of Reference librarianship.
2. Many Reference librarians feel that their duties are limited to provide reference tools, but not to answer their queries. Reference librarian should discard such feelings. They will extend their service to provide reader's service.
3. It is generally said that library's role is to issue and return of the books. This is an old concept. Now

Reference librarian solves all problems of the reader and provides reading material of reader's choice. Librarian should change their attitude of a traditional librarian as we are marching ahead towards digital library.

4. If there comes only few readers, we should go into search of the reason and should prove a true librarian to imporve readership.
5. Reference librarian should concentrate on giving answer of the queries of the reader considering the importance, adequacy and time taken.
6. Librarians should leave the old views and discard old pattern. It disheartens the young librarians. Reference librarian should adopt new patterns, and modern reference tools.

4 Initiation to Newcomers/ Fresh Readers

Readers – Several readers enter the library. They come without any restriction of caste, creed and colour. They vary in nature, attitude. Their demand is different. Their queries are different which require different reading material and reference tools.

Newcomer – There are many readers who enter the library. They are not aware of the functioning of the library. They do not know about the reading material kept in the library. It is necessary to make the newcomer aware of different departments, collection, techniques, rules and regulations and services rendered by the library, so that he may consult the library independently.

Library – Library is a social institution. Hence it should be utilized by the whole society. There are many systems, equipments which are used in administration and organization and should be known by the new readers, such as:

(a) Circulation section

(b) Acquisition section

(c) Reference section

(d) Documentation section

All these departments are directly related to the readers. Newcomer should be given a knowledge of each department, their location working and functions. Every department should have its name plate. Newcomer is a guest or the customer and he should be welcome by the librarian with the words "What can I do for you", "I welcome you, Sir", "May I help you", "Kindly allow me to make you aware about library working."

This type of dealing encourages the readers. Librarian's behaviour counts much. Librarian should be soft-spoken and of sweet nature.

(A) CIRCULATION SECTION

It is also known as lending department. It has a counter with two windows — one for charging (issue) work and another for discharging (return) work. This department has its rules and regulations. It has fixed hours for its activities, which are fixed by considering many aspects like — reader's choice, staff convenience and the working hours of parental body. There are rules of membership, days for issue and return of the book, reading facilities, reservation facilities, number of books to be borrowed, etc.

Newcomer should be given knowledge of all such rules.

(B) ACQUISITION DEPARTMENT (SECTION)

This department undertakes the work of selection, ordering, purchasing of documents. It also deals with accessioning of documents. This department has no direct concern with the reader because all works other than selection of books are not related to the reader. Selection procedure involves the suggestions of the reader.

Newcomer should be aware with the functions of Acquisition Section.

(C) REFERENCE SECTION

This section has a wide area of work. It is directly related to the readers. This department meets the reader first when they enter the library. Reference librarian welcomes the reader and makes him known with the functions of this department. Reference librarian answers the queries of the reader. It has a Reference Desk/Counter which provides reader's service. All short range informations are prepared in a reference diary. Reference Section actively works and give necessary directions to the reader to consult reference tools. It also provides a copy of the rules of the library to the reader which are to be followed them. These rules cover a layout picture of the library, its sections, working of the sections, systems of circulation, time and the persons to whom readers should approach for their problems, rules also cover the type and specificity of collections.

(D) DOCUMENTATION SECTION

This is an important department. It generally works in university, research and special libraries. In such libraries researchers require special services like bibliographies, documentation list, indexes and abstracts, translation service, reprographic service and automation service. A newcomer is given full knowledge of this section so that he can search the literature of his choice, trace himself, or put his demand for it. In modern libraries Documentation section is known as an important department. The services of this department are very important to the newcomer.

In view of the above, the newcomer needs help and librarian/library staff provide him all facilities so that he may be attracted towards the library for its maximum use.

Reference Service in Various Libraries

5

Reference service is similar in every library as reference procedures and techniques are the same. There is a need of reference librarian in all libraries, who should be a well-qualified person. There may be different types of reference tools in all libraries according to the nature and objectives of library.

Similarity

(1) Readers/users utilize reference service in a similar way.

(2) Readers/users present their queries.

(3) Reference service are collected and arranged in every library.

Differences

1. *Nature of the readers* – Readers vary in nature. They are different in sex, colour and creed. They have different behaviour. They may be businessmen in industrial libraries, scientists in research libraries, students in college libraries, technicians in technical libraries and any social man in public libraries.
2. *Difference in nature of questions* – As readers are of different nature, their questions are also different. Their problems are also different.
3. *Difference in timings* – All type of libraries have different timings according to the needs of the readers/users.

4. *Difference in sources* – Every library has its limited resources and it is their efforts to purchase the best in lowest budget and according to the needs of the readers. Libraries are of many kinds and different nature of readers and their problems. Hence, there are different sources also.

(A) PUBLIC LIBRARIES

Public libraries are established by the public, with the public fund, and for the public. Readers of all communities without consideration of caste, colour and creed, can use the library and utilize its resources. Any person of the society can be the member of the public libraries. Readers are divided on the basis of their education, functions, activities, age, income and subject of their choice. Readers may be categorised in other way also like teachers, students, scientists, businessmen, research scholars, politicians, engineers, inventors, musicians, social welfare workers, etc. Readers consult the library freely and without any restriction but follow library rules.

In every field whether it is business, industries, science or social science there is continuous knowledge expansion. Informations are always useful to people. Reference librarian always makes efforts to come in contact with the readers. All facilities are provided for study and learning which are published daily in newspapers. Public library subscribes all such newspapers and journals and houses them for consultation of the readers. Library also makes the readers aware of new journals received from time to time. In fact readers do not know what type of information and material is available in the library and which query may be answered. There are some readers who have limited themselves to just reading in library while they can be served by the library for any information they want.

Reference service has importance in a public library. In earlier period there were only few libraries which could give reference service. But with the increasing demand of the readers every library has started providing reference service. It is the duty of Reference librarian to respond to the queries of the readers and help them in making the information and information sources available to the readers. There are few libraries which have started modern techniques of reference service. There are four factors to be considered for effective reference service:

(a) Intelligent mind

(b) Adequate collection

(c) Reference sources

(d) Coordination among (a), (b) and (c).

It fact many states have promulgated Public Library Act. They have good collection of the reference tools. But they do not have reference librarian. Librarian who is supposed to provide reference service, is busy with many tasks and tight schedule. Some do not have reference tools. This has resulted in a limited reference service to the readers and a slow progress in reference service.

Questions to be put up

(a) There are questions which have fact-finding and permanent answer. Such answers are given immediately. There are less chances of different answers. Such questions are common and presented by majority of the readers. Such questions are based on principles and systems, and we call them Direct Reference Service.

(b) Second type of questions need thinking. Reference librarian thinks and applies his intelligentsia while giving answers. Such questions are not answered immediately and directions are given by consulting reference books. It takes time to get the answer of the question. Generally such questions are put by the students and technicians.

(c) Third type of questions are answered with reference tools. Reader should be aware of reference books and their special features so that he can search the answer of the query independently. Such reference tools are:

(1) Reader's guide to bibliographies

(2) Catalogue or dictionaries

Size and Expansion of Library

Reference service is given according to the size of the library. Small libraries are not supposed to give reference service and organize separate Reference desk, Reference document, etc. Librarian is supposed to provide reference service. Readers also put up simple queries which are to be answered within limited resources. It is suggested that small libraries should retain the periodicals stock for a period of 5 years. Librarian should have the knowledge of the collection of other libraries of other district and regional libraries.

The size of a library is evaluated on the basis of the resources of the library. The library having limited resources cannot acquire reference sources. Such libraries purchase low cost reference books which could give general informations for general readers. Librarian keeps in touch with the readers of general taste and relating to local areas. Small libraries arrange following reference service:

(a) Selection of important reference books.

(b) Arrangement of circulation and technical work at one place, so that reader can be dealt at one place.

(c) Display of bibliographies and journals.

(d) Maintaining the file of current issues of journals and newspapers.

The other type of libraries are large libraries which have separate Reference department. Large libraries cover the large area. They have ample resources. Generally such libraries are established in cities of more than 20,000 population but in India the cities of 1 lakh population have libraries with reference department. These libraries have reference assistance in addition to librarian. Generally all libraries have reference assistance in addition to librarian. Generally all libraries purchase reference books. In large libraries Reference department has a separate existence and is organized as a separate department in a systematic way. It has the following sources:

(a) Reference desk

(b) Reference diary

(c) Separate stack for reference books.

(d) Separate seating arrangement for readers to consult reference books.

(e) Selection of reference books.

(f) Well-experienced and trained reference librarian.

(g) Preparation for reference queries.

Reference Staff

Library staff depends on the size and collection of libraries. Small library will hardly have reference librarian while large library has Reference librarian along with other reference staff. Reference librarian is supposed to be an experienced and trained person having wide knowledge of reference books. He should be intelligent, farsighted and psychologist. He should prepare reference diary and note down important but common queries of the readers and their answers.

There are a few staff formulas:

ALA staff formula

Small library	- 1/8 of the total staff
Large library	- 1/5 of the total staff
Trained Reference staff	- 1/8 of the total reference staff.

Building

Reference Department needs special building suited to reference service. This department should be organized near the entrance gate. Reference window should be at central place in Reference department to facilitate the readers. Reference counter should be placed near the reference department. Reference books should be properly arranged on the shelf and represented by guides and indicators. There should be seating arrangement for readers.

Open Access System

Open Access System is an important factor for consideration in public libraries. Proper shelf arrangement according to the choice of readers is essential for reference service. There is a saying in Arabic: "Open book provides open thinking". Open

Access System helps the reader in tracing his book. There is a saving in staff and less number of staff can manage the reference service because of less number of queries as the readers search information of many queries independently in Open Access System. Reference books should be open to all for consultation so that readers may use them fully and freely.

Telephone Service

There are two types of services:

(a) *Through telephone service* – There are many libraries which install public telephone in the campus so that the readers may use them for getting their information without wasting time.

(b) *Through telephone service with reference librarian* – This telephone is used by reference librarian to answer the queries of the readers and it saves the time of the reader.

(B) ACADEMIC LIBRARIES

Academic library provides very important reference service. Such libraries are university, college, and school libraries. All academic libraries provide reference service of the same nature but it differs in reference tools, their specialities and the area.

School Library

School libraries house collection on regional basis. Collection is more or less related to geography, history and social problems. Such reference tools help the children in developing their qualities and intelligentisia. Collection includes atlas, globe, maps, dictionary, pictorial encyclopedia, etc. There are precautions to be taken when selecting the reference tools, such as:

(a) Foreign reference books to be avoided.

(b) Indian reference books should be purchased in single copy.

(c) More costly reference books should be avoided unless they are very useful.

(d) More weightage should be given to dictionaries,

handbooks, encyclopedias, biographies, grammar books, translations, etc.

(e) More pictorial books should be purchased.

Examples

(a) Children's Knowledge of Universe
(b) Oxford Junior Encyclopedia
(c) Chamber's Encyclopedia
(d) Newn's Pictorial Knowledge
(e) Encyclopedia for Children
(f) Oxford Dictionary
(g) English Pronunciation Dictionary
(h) Sources of English Words and Phrases
(i) Oxford Atlas
(j) Survey of India Maps
(k) Survey of India Dictionary
(l) Chambers Biographical Dictionary
(m) Dictionary of National Biography
(n) Pearles Encyclopedia
(o) Times of India Directory
(p) Discovery Books
(q) Every Day Life Series

Bibliographies

(r) Books for Young People
(s) Under Eleven Children's Catalogue
(t) Enjoying Science Books for School Libraries
(u) The Use of Books (Nelson)
(v) Catalogues of Children Book Trust, Atmaram, Rajkamal, Rajpal, Sasta Sahitya Mandal.

Hindi Books

(a) सचित्र विश्वकोष
(b) संसार ज्ञान
(c) हिन्दुस्तान समाचार

Management

Reference service should be managed properly. Racks should not be more than 4 feet high and kept with reading tables. Some reading tables have attached racks of two shelves. These tables should be arranged according to the nature of the reference books. C.H.C. Oshan suggested that shelf should have depth of 1' 2", height 3" and shelfs 3 or 4 in number. Lower shelf should be used for maps.

Reference books should be classified according to the nature of the reference books. Every shelf should have shelf guides and shelf indicators.

Finance

There is hardly any amount for reference service in school libraries. The budget for reference books should be fixed for reference service and reference books. Reference books should be properly bound as children roughly handle the books.

College Library

College libraries serve the undergraduate and postgraduate students. Students, when admitted in a college first enquire about the library and its rules and regulations to be a member of the library and its use. They enquire about the collection, systems, and procedure of lending. There is separate reference department in each college. Reference department has more importance in European countries. Every college library is equipped with reference department in European countries. In India college libraries have reference department but not properly managed because of unqualified staff, inadequate collection and lack of finance. But during the 21st century college libraries have developed Reference departments equipped with adequate reference books. Reference librarians are being appointed to serve the reader efficiently.

Reference department acquires collection relating to the course and general studies. Students study many subjects and participate in competitions, debates, seminars, etc. and take the help of the library at every point of study. Reference service helps them in their studies. Reference departments have organized a reference window where queries of the readers are answered.

University Library

University library provides reference service of higher level as researchers are conducted in universities. Readers include teachers, research scholars. All standard reference books are purchased and housed in reference department. Well-qualified and trained reference librarian is appointed. Reference department is developed as an important department in university library.

All important reference books are acquired in reference department of university library, such as:

(a) *Encyclopedia Britannica*
(b) *Encyclopedia Americana*
(c) *Webster's Dictionary*
(d) *International Yearbook*
(e) *Year Book and Who's Who*
(f) *Oxford Atlas*
(g) *International Yearbook*
(h) *Encyclopedia of Social Sciences*
(i) *Life Science Abstract*
(j) *Chemical Abstract*
(k) *Encyclopedia Bibliographies*
(l) *Encyclopedia of Religion*
(m) *Webster's International Dictionary*
(n) *Oxford English Dictionary*
(o) *Encyclopedia of Science and Technology*
(p) *Encyclopedia of Library & Information Science*
(q) *World Atlas*
(r) *Books in Print*
(s) *British Books in Print*
(t) *Indian Books in Print*
(u) *University Hand Book*
(v) *Ulritch International Periodical Directory*
(w) *India, a Reference Annual*

All the above reference books are generally selected in university libraries. Reference books are fully used in such libraries. All students generally study higher education and indulge in research work and utilize reference service in the development of their education and knowledge growth. There are other tools also which help in reference service like cataloguing based on standard catalogue code and classification based on standard classification scheme. Open Access System is followed. There is telephone service in addition to fax and e-mail services. Faculty members, students and research scholars take benefit of all facilities provided by the university library. Reference librarian helps them in tracing their information. Maximum number of readers trace their information and consult the reference tools independently.

Microfilm and photostat equipment also support the reference service. The other services which are very important and necessary in university libraries are SDI and CAS services which are provided to the readers. Such services provide uptodate information to research scholars and the students. These services are somehow costly, but essential in university libraries. NISCAIR (Previously INSDOC) provides all such services also.

Organization

The organization of Reference department depends on the nature of Reference service. Reference department or the Reference library may be divided in three parts, *i.e.* pure science, social science and humanities. Though it will be more expensive because there are reference books used in more than one part and separate copy of reference book will be purchased for each part. But this may be avoided by reference librarian giving directions to the readers.

Reference service more or less depend on the organization of the Reference department. Its services should be centralized. There may be more than one Reference librarian. Their duties should be managed in such a way that reference services should run smoothly. Reference librarian should be aware of reference books so that all queries should be answered properly. Reference department prepares bibliographies in many languages. Translation service is also provided to the readers.

University library renders the following three types of services:

(a) Reference service to students,

(b) Reference service to faculty,

(c) Reference service to research scholars.

Reference service to students is given relating to books, information regarding courses, extra curricular informations and queries are answered. There are books which are not in accordance with courses but very useful to the students for their wider knowledge. There are course books but not upto the standard. Reference librarian helps them in providing suitable books.

For example, a student asked some questions about total matches and number of goals of Shri Dhyan Chand, vizard of Hockey in India. Reference library suggested *Who's Who in India* and *Biography of Dhyan Chand.* However, there are students of different nature, mind and different in queries.

Faculty also needs reference service, *i.e.* university statistics, their courses, teaching techniques, trade catalogues of publishers, and journals and published articles. Besides this translation, lists of specific subjects, list of unpublished books, preparation of bibliography are provided by the Reference department.

Research scholars also need reference service provided by the Reference librarian. Most of the research scholars search their information by themselves. But Reference librarian's services are also very much necessary to research scholars with the help of books-in-print, subject bibliography, British National bibliography, Indian National bibliography, literacy supplement, reviews, list of unpublished books, microfilm list, subject abstract etc.

Sometimes library fails to provide required reading material to research scholars. Reference librarian provide such material through inter library loan service.

(C) SPECIAL LIBRARIES

Special libraries are supposed to be an information centers. These libraries mainly provide reference service and provide specific informations to scientists. Special libraries have special collections as these libraries provide reading material relating to research material. These libraries are generally established in industrial and business houses, scientific institutions, medical science, engineering institutions, etc.

Special libraries provide subject bibliographies and directories and make them available under inter-library loan. Such libraries organize their reference departments in many parts, such as:

(a) Photo section (microfilm, photostat, reading)
(b) Translation section
(c) Reference section (bibliographies, indexing, abstracting, etc.)
(d) Computer section
(e) Information desk
(f) Documentation section

Special libraries access subject reference books and related bibliographies, index, abstracts and translation lists. Readers are informed about latest arrivals through information bulletins. Libraries made necessary survey of related other libraries and their special collection to provide efficient reference service. Libraries subscribe specific subject newspapers and maintain chip files based on research problems. Indian Institute of World Affairs maintains clip files of newspapers of 21 countries and provides reference service. This clip files are arranged subjectwise. It is a special service. This library also selects survey reports, meeting proceedings, committee reports of the Govt., Board's reports, etc. All this material is useful to the research scholars and educationists. Reference librarian helps them in tracing their information. They make them aware of library systems and rules and regulations of the library. Library also organizes seminars, symposiums, lectures to create awareness among the readers about the utility and service of the library.

Organization of Reference Section/Department

6

Reference section is important in a library. Its organization has much importance. There is a need of proper organization of reference section for the smooth running and library development. In small libraries Reference Department has no separate existence. Librarian also works as Reference librarian because of small number of readers and collection. But in large libraries Reference Section is organized as separate unit to serve the readers properly and efficiently.

Library is a growing organization. It is possible when all sections of a library work smoothly and satisfy the readers. Therefore, Reference Section should be organized in a planned way with all precautions and considering all prerequisites, such as:

(a) Location of Reference Section
(b) Reference librarian and staff
(c) Reference sources
(d) Reference Service and Referral Service
(e) Reference Records
(f) Evaluation

(A) LOCATION OF REFERENCE SECTION

The main aim of the Reference Section is to serve the readers and satisfy them to their maximum satisfaction. In small libraries, reference service is provided on lending counter. In large libraries Reference Section is located near the stack area and the catalogue. Some readers are of the opinion that reference counter should be near the gate so that the readers should put their problems before Reference librarian before he moves for other sections. It is a matter of discussion as how much accommodation the Reference Department requires. There are standards at National and International level to decide the location of the library, working of the library and job specifications. There are standards of library furniture, building equipments, air-conditioning and lighting, etc.

It considers the provision of Reference Desk which is necessary for effective reference service. It is a half-round table attached with a special shelf keeping the important reference service. There is a specialized reference stack area housing the important reference tools required for long range reference service and Document Delivery service.

(B) REFERENCE LIBRARIAN AND STAFF

Dr. S.R. Ranganathan says "Reference librarian has potential to study reference books and giving the answer of the queries of the readers. He always encourages his colleagues and motivate them to respond to the readers demand.

However, Reference librarian should be well educated, trained and studious and capable to deal with the readers to search their informations.

The library should be equipped with a separate Reference librarian. The staff should be appointed on the basis of the number of readers attend the Reference department.

University Grants Commission has made provisions for the post of Reference librarian in university libraries. It was recommended by Library Advisory Committee headed by Dr. Ranganathan in 1959. Reference librarian will be similar to Reader's post in the university. According to Ranganathan a Reference librarian should have qualities of Ram, Lakshman, Bharat and Shatrughan. Shatrughan was not proudy. He worshipped the 'kharaon' for 14 years and helped his elder brother Bharat. Bharat was dedicated to his elder brother Ram. He managed the kingdom with honesty and served the public though he was not king. Lakshman was a man of dedication and a blind follower of the king Ram. He was not selfish. He followed Ram and never personal thought of any wrong or right.

Similarly, Reference librarian should be honest and loyal to the public.

Reference Department is the backbone of a library. There are requisites for a successful Reference staff:

(a) Knowledge of reference books,

(b) Love for readers,

(c) Willingness to serve,

(d) Organising capacity,

(e) Soft spoken and tactful,

(f) Presence of mind.

In short, a Reference librarian and Reference Assistants should be well-known to library techniques, systems, reference sources, more than two languages, subject knowledge, human psychology and also work with service feeling, good behaviour. They should be educated and trained also.

(C) REFERENCE SOURCES

There is a need of good and standard reference books in a large library for his successful functioning. It depends on the nature, status, economic sources and type of libraries. Such factors determine the number and kinds of reference sources. But there should be a balanced collection of reference books in a library. Reference sources may be Encyclopedia, Dictionaries, Annual Report, Biographies, Citation Index, Gazetteers, Yearbooks, Handbooks and Almanacs, etc. Special and research libraries acquire Bibliographies, Index and Abstracts, etc.

(D) REFERENCE SERVICE AND REFERRAL SERVICE

While organizing a Reference Department more emphasis should be given to reference and referral services. What services are to be rendered to the readers will be based on kinds of readers, status of readers, types of library and financial resources. Reference department provides following reference services:

(a) Guidance
(b) Advisory service
(c) Quick service
(d) Consultation service
(e) Documentation service
(f) Document delivery service
(g) Referral service.

(E) REFERENCE RECORDS

All possible questions and informations should be recorded in reference diary. Such questions and information should be based on the following aspects:

(a) Common questions.
(b) Common nature of readers.
(c) General problems of researches being conducted in the institutes.
(d) Common informations to be answered immediately.
(e) Local problems and environments.

Such record is very much useful for ready reference service.

(F) EVALUATION

Any service evaluation depends on the following factors:

(a) Objective of the service.
(b) Readers choice.
(c) Continuous consultation with the reader.
(d) Satisfaction of the readers.
(e) Reference service, how much effective it is.
(f) Bibliometrics of readers queries. How many questions could not be answered and why.
(g) Categories of the readers. Readers guided, consulted, answered, satisfied.

Sources of Information

7

Information sources means — Information + Sources. In ordinary language information sources indicates to the new facts and new subject or information. But in Modern Scientific language information is known as new knowledge which has special qualities which are related to specific subject, facts and events.

Modern age is a period of knowledge explosion. Millions of articles and lakhs of books are published every month. There is a problem of search of the desired information out of the whole knowledge. There are many checks to control the knowledge explosion. Reference sources are the media of information. Information sources are related to subjects. These cannot be limited to a particular subject. They have wider information.

(A) CLASSIFICATION OF INFORMATION SOURCES

Educationists are not of one opinion about the classification of information sources. Dr. Ranganathan has categorized information sources in 4 categories:

(a) Conventional documents,

(b) Neo-Conventional documents,

(c) Non-Conventional documents,

(d) Meta-documents.

(a) Conventional Documents

Such documents or information sources which are traditionally used during previous years are called conventional documents. There were clay tablets, papyrus, etc. used before the invention of paper production and printing technology.

There were no systematic publications on information sources. They were not written with this object of reference service except catalogues.

(b) Neo-conventional Documents

Neo-conventional documents include various standards, patents, specifications data of properties, reaction formulas, press cuttings of base material on social sciences and sciences. In this way various patents, standards and specifications which are generated are known as Neo-conventional documents.

(c) Non-conventional Documents

Such documents are neither conventional nor neo-conventional. They are different from other documents. They include new developments, new data, events and scientific formulas prepared with new techniques. Non-conventional documents can be categorised as under:

(1) Audio documents

(2) Visual documents

(3) Audio-video documents

(4) Micro copy

(d) Meta Documents

These documents are prepared with new scientific techniques without the help of manual labour, *i.e.* technology, photocopy, radar, network, communication channel and latest informations are preserved in it. For example: CD, Network, Fax, E-mail, etc.

However, Dr. Ranganathan categorized the documents based on physical features. They are not considered based on knowledge and information.

Grogan and Hannson have categorized documents on the basis of information. Grogan has divided documents in categories while Hannson has categorised in three categories:

According to Hannson:

(a) **Primary sources** – It includes books, periodicals, reports, proceeding, seminar reports, commercial literature, standards, etc.

(b) **Secondary sources** – It includes index, abstracts, bibliographies, reviews, surveys, etc.

Grogan has categorized the documents in three categories which is based on knowledge and information:

(a) Primary sources,

(b) Secondary sources,

(c) Tertiary sources.

(B) PRIMARY SOURCES

There are information sources which include informations of researches and developments. In other words all such facts, truth, informations which are published for the first time and based on fundamental research and primary survey. The documents in which such informations are published, are known as primary sources, such informations are not available in secondary sources. Primary sources are not organized themselves. They originally have primary informations. It has more importance in researches, theses, reports, proceedings, etc.

Primary sources have following kinds of documents:

(a) **Books** – All books are not treated as primary sources. Only such books are known as primary sources which have new thoughts. Example: *Five Laws of Library Science.*

(b) **Periodicals** – Only such periodicals are known as primary sources which have fundamental and new information generated and reports. Periodicals are generally weekly, fortnightly, quarterly, monthly, half-yearly, yearly, etc. Periodicals includes magazines, bulletins, reports, reviews, articles, research reviews.

(c) **Patents** – When a person invents a new technique, product formula, he needs his monopoly and keeps his rights with him. Government approves such monopoly as patent. Therefore, patent is an authority letter of the Government which gives all rights of using such invention to the inventor.

Patent is a primary source. It gives detailed report and description about the invention. Such patents are published in Government Gazette.

Standards – Standards are such documents in which some specifications of a particular product or service are standardized by the Government such as quality and quantity of industrial products, size, kinds, process, working and terminology rules and regulations. Standards are very important and useful for consumers as they purchase or consume such products with faith and belief. Generally standards are the handbook or bulletin which represents details of the items approved by the "Bureau of Indian Standards," New Delhi.

Standards may be categorized as under:

(a) Quality standards,

(b) Evaluation standards,

(c) Terminology standards,

(d) Weights and measures standards.

Research monograph – It is a report published on a fundamental research which may produce the principles and fundamentals applied by the author before the research. Such monographs are very useful for guidance of research work.

Research reports – Research and development informations are published for highlighting them. Such reports provide necessary information regarding researches being done in the same subjects. Informations in research reports are more effective and fundamentally important. These reports are very useful in modern time when researches are being done in good number and such reports have been useful as media of communication, extension and expansion.

Conference proceedings – Conference proceedings are such articles which are presented in National and International conferences and seminars and they are proved as a source of information. All such articles are related to new researches and investigations. They include conclusions and results and fact-finding which are published or mentioned in research projects beforehand to their publication in periodicals.

Theses – These documents are fundamental work in a specific subject. Universities award Ph.D. degree on their approval or authenticity examined by the subject experts.

Theses are also published by the researches or the institutions which highlight techniques, methods, procedures and principles for others' guidance. But most of the theses are not published and hence their benefits do not reach the society.

Unpublished sources – There are many unpublished sources among the primary sources which are very useful for information. These are letters, portraits, coins, memoranda, engraving pieces, and other hand-written bulletin and handbook, company files which are of fundamental importance and prove useful for consumers and researchers.

(C) SECONDARY SOURCES

These are such sources which have fundamental or basic informations. These are prepared and provide basic informations in a planned way. Secondary sources present general informations instead of basic or fundamental informations. Moreover, in such sources informations given in primary sources are collected, selected and arranged properly and grouped together.

Mr. Bonn has categorized secondary sources in three categories:

(a) Indexing type (Index, bibliography, abstracting, etc.)

(b) Survey type (Reviews, treatise, etc.)

(c) Reference type (Encyclopedia, handbooks, etc.)

(a) Abstracting and Indexing Periodicals

Abstracting periodicals provide new and current informations to scientists and technicians and such informations are related to technical progress and developments in the field of science and technology. Indexing periodicals are the source of specific informations and provide up to date informations. These are such secondary sources which help in researches.

(b) Reviews of Progress

The difficulties found in indexing and abstracting resulted into search in review literature. When a researcher cannot find the fact or does not understand the abstract of an article or other item, he goes for consultation for review literature to get proper explanation or views about the item. It is a secondary source in which academicians or scholars highlight the development and progress of a specific subject and such informations are very useful to the research scientists and students.

(c) Reference Books

These are secondary sources. These are prepared on the basis of primary sources which include informations regarding facts, knowledge, events and explanations.

Reference books can be arranged in a sequence as under:

(a) Encyclopedia
(b) Dictionary
(c) Handbook
(d) Tables

(d) Subject Books

Subject books are such books which are different from reference books. Those books describe and arrange a subject or subjects. Such books help the reader in studying the fundamentals of a subject. These may be enumerated as under:

(a) Treatise
(b) Monograph
(c) Textbooks

(D) TERTIARY SOURCES

These sources are valuable and important to search the primary and secondary sources. These are prepared with the help of secondary sources. Some tertiary sources are as under:

(a) Directory
(b) Yearbook
(c) Guides to Literature
(d) Bibliography of bibliographies
(e) List of Research in progress

(a) Directory

Directories provide informations of special type and in specific area of subject. These include informations regarding persons, institutions, their address, products, national and international organizations, their activities, etc. which are helpful to the readers of any nature and type.

Directory is a list of persons or organizations systematically arranged, usual in alphabetic or classified order, giving address, affiliations, for individuals, and addresses, officers, functions and similar data of organization.

(b) Yearbook

Yearbook provides informations of a nation, region, etc. and is published yearly. It includes informations of events, awards, addresses, etc. arranged according to subjects. It has an index at the end.

(c) Guide to Literature

Guides represents the matter relating to basic information of subject. These guides also mention the descriptive photos, tables, diagrams, etc. to explain the information or detail of the item or subject. Readers are helped in searching their subject literature of their choice.

(d) Bibliography of Bibliographies

Bibliography is a systematic description and history of books, their authoship, printing, publishing, editions, etc. It is a list of books of a particular author, printer or country or those dealing with any particular theme, the literature or the subject. A bibliography may include a detailed description of the books themselves and in this sense the bibliographer requires a knowledge not only of the history of typography but also of book-binding and paper-making. A bibliography may be a author bibliography, critical bibliography and bibliography of bibliographies.

List of Research in Progress

There are different researchers working on different aspects of a subject in different areas. There are a few researchers working on the same project which is a repetition and wastage of energy. This overlapping may be avoided by publishing the reports of progress of researches being currently done. This information may be circulated. This enables a new researcher to know about the researches being conducted. This can avoid duplication of research.

NISCAIR (National Institute of Science Communication and Information Research) (previously known as INSDOC) has published "Current Research Projects in CSIR Laboratories," and "Directory of Scientific Research in Indian Universities"; AIU (Association of Indian Universities) has published a bibliography of researches awarded by the universities of India.

Evaluation of Reference Books

8

The handwritten or printed writings are called books with no consideration of size, and number of pages. Books have wide scope. They include all type of reading material grouped together or collection of thoughts of one persons or a team of authors. They fulfil the objective of reading, learning, entertainment, specific readings and informations.

Books are of many kinds, *i.e.* reference books, textbooks, treatise, classics, monographs, etc. We deal here with reference books.

Reference Books

Reference books are such books which are used for some particular information. These are different from treatise, monographs, classics. These are used for micro-studies. They provide authentic information and answer of readers' queries.

As a glossary explains that reference books are such books which help the reader with their description arrangements and quality of information, they are consulted always by the readers for any or every problem. But they are mostly consulted in the campus of the library as they are costly and bulky and generally in volumes. These are read continuously and consulted during general studies and research. These provide specific informations.

Information Reference Books

(1) Encyclopedia

(2) Directories

(3) Dictionary

(4) Yearbook
(5) Almanac
(6) Biography
(7) Handbook
(8) Bibliography
(9) Geographical sources (Atlas, globe)
(10) Index
(11) Abstract
(12) Periodicals
(13) Audio-visual aids
(14) Union catalogue

(A) EVALUATION

Reference tools are important and provide valuable informations to readers. If a reader does not access the relevant and useful informations, the objective of reference books is defeated. There is a knowledge explosion and millions of books are being produced each year. Reference tools are necessary which can guide a researcher to trace the book of his choice and also to provide necessary information he wants. Thus, it is a challenging step for a library to select the suitable, adequate and most useful reference books in the library. Reference librarian selects the reference books after consultation and careful scrutiny.

There are seven stages of evaluation of reference books:

(a) Purpose
(b) Authority
(c) Scope
(d) Treatment
(e) Arrangement
(f) Format
(g) Special features

(a) Purpose – This is the first step of evaluation. The objective of the reference book should be evaluated. It is to be seen what objective is fulfilled by the reference book. It can be evaluated by the title, subject, thought contents, introduction and preface.

(b) Authority – Authenticity is an important quality of a reference book and it requires a fact-finding and adequate information. Authority can be evaluated on the basis of these factors:

(1) Author of the book

(2) Editor of the book

(3) Compiler of the book

(4) Translator of the book

(5) Publisher of the book

(6) Distributor of the book

(7) Origin of the book

If the author, translator, editor, or the compiler is an important person of his subject field and well-known academician, it will prove the reference book as a useful tool. In the same manner publisher and distributor are also considered for the standard of the reference book. A well-known and a standard publisher will never publish a below standard book. The well-known and standard distributor will not take the responsibility of distributing the below standard reference book.

(c) Scope – Every reference book has an area of study which may be a general or specific area. A reference book of a specific area and specific subject with specific information is always preferred. Hence, a reference book may be evaluated on the basis of its scope of area. Scope may be:

(1) Area

(2) Region

(3) Period

(4) Subject

(5) Information

We can concise them in two categories:

(1) Subject coverage

(2) Subject range.

(d) Treatment – Every reference book has its specific writing style, language behaviour, and explanatory method which makes a reference book qualitative. Therefore, all above qualities may be checked and evaluated while selecting a reference book. These components are as under:

(1) Writing style

(2) Current informations

(3) Fact finding and adequacy of informations

(4) Reliability of informations

(5) Clarity of informations

(6) Standard of informations

(7) Clarity of language.

(e) Arrangement – Information should be arranged in such a way that it should be easily traced. Informations are arranged alphabetically, classified chronologically and geographically in reference books. Arrangement may be any but it should be so perfect that information may be traced without wasting any time. This is possible if informations are arranged in helpful order. Reference book should have an index at the end as it will supplement the help to trace the information.

(f) Format – Reference books have different physical format, *i.e.* binding, paper used for printing, printing style and impression. A standard reference book has good binding and attractive printing, such as:

(1) Outer physique should be attractive

(2) Binding should be attractive

(3) Superfine printing

(4) Super quality paper.

(g) Special Features – Reference books have variety of information presented in different form and presentation. There are reference books having similar information but only one reference book is selected from among them though they have similar informations. It is necessary to see that the reference book selected should have some specific features in comparison with other reference books. Special features include:

(1) Frequency of publication regularly
(2) Type of index
(3) All important informations are included
(4) Articles are written with some object
(5) Readers are satisfied

(B) MODEL FOR EVALUATING REFERENCE BOOKS

(a) Complete title, sub-title
(b) Authoritative informations:
  (1) Author and collaborators
  (2) Publishers and their address
  (3) Place of publication
  (4) Year of publication
(c) Edition:
  (1) First edition year
  (2) Present edition year
  (3) Total number of volume
(d) Subject area:
  (1) Object
  (2) Subject matter
  (3) Type of material
  (4) Scope of information
(e) Presentation style (treatment):
  (1) Information new or old
  (2) Informations reliable or unreliable
  (3) Information clear or prejudiced
  (4) Utility of information:
    (i) General readers

(ii) Special readers

(iii) Children.

(f) Arrangement:

(1) Alphabetical

(2) Classified

(3) Geographical

(4) Chronological.

(g) Outer form:

(1) Binding

(2) Printing

(3) Pictorial.

(h) Other special features.

Reference Service and New Developments

9

This is an age of knowledge explosion. There is continuous publications of books, periodicals, articles, seminar papers, conference proceedings, agreements, treatises, and reports every day. It is the duty of Reference librarian to provide reading material and their informations through various sources. Reference service has accepted this challenge. Reference service has a wide scope. It is not sufficient to organize the reference department and complete the duty by giving guidance to the readers. But it is more necessary to provide up to date and current informations and applying new techniques for the purpose. There have been many developments to prepare and publish bibliographies, indexes, abstracts and also provide translation service, reprographic services, etc. The latest development is computer services which is also known as automation services.

(A) INDEXING SERVICES

Bone says: "Index is an alphabetical list of the names, words, places and subject terms along with page of a complete book and document." Therefore, indexing is a source which works as a chain between the subject and related document. It is a classified directory of various articles and thoughts of a document. Indexing services are useful to the researcher and the readers to search the required information. It saves the time and labour of researcher. It is very important as:

(a) It is a list of documents or micro-document (Micro thoughts)

(b) It is alphabetical

(c) It has bibliographical details
(d) It is based on indexing terms
(e) It is prepared according to some standard systems
(f) It is time saving
(g) It saves labour
(h) It is a reference source.

Preparing entries for an index is called indexing. It is an important technique. Computers are also used for indexing purpose. All documents concerning books and non-book material, macro thoughts and micro thoughts are access to computer software which select and include only important and related terms for indexing purpose and arrange them alphabetically. Base terms and general terms are shown separately in bold letters and small letters. Computer service is very useful for indexing work and also provides indexing services.

(B) ABSTRACTING

Today there is a tremendous progress in the field of science and technology. The related literature is being published in more than 50 languages in more than 174 countries and it is a continuous process. Periodicals in more than 1 lakh in number are being published every year in the field of science and technology and includes more than 5 lakhs of articles which are very much useful in the field of science and technology. This trend of publications in millions have caused a problem before the researchers to trace the required information. Libraries and information centers check this knowledge explosion through bibliographic control, indexing and abstracting. Reference librarians make them aware with the up to date and current reference and information sources.

Abstracting service plays an important role in modern world of knowledge explosion. There are many abstracts which are being published in every field of subject and are providing up to date informations. Current contents provide current information. Such services are provided by the reference department. Abstract means — Index + Summary (abstract) of the micro thought provided. Example: Chemical abstract,

Biological abstract, Psychological abstract, etc. There are more than 1000 abstracts being published in various fields of subject and circulated throughout the world and serving the scientists and researchers. Researcher or the reader goes through the abstract of the article or other micro thought and select his required information. It saves the time as the reader need not to go through the whole of the article. He just goes through the summary (abstract) of the article and decides whether it is needed by him.

Mainly, abstracts are of two kinds:

(i) Indicative abstract

(ii) Informative abstract.

(i) **Indicative abstract** – In this abstract the control theme is highlighted about the subject or thoughts of the author. It highlights the nature of the document and area of study. It helps the researcher whether the document is helpful to him or not.

(ii) **Informative abstract** – In this abstract all important details, facts and necessary data are presented or highlighted. It has more detail than the indicative abstract.

Utility of Abstracting

(a) It saves the time of the researcher.

(b) Abstract is provided in the common language understandable to the readers.

(c) It gives facilities to select the information of his choice.

(d) Abstracts may be translated as the information given in abstract is authentic.

Important Abstracts in India

(a) Indian Education Abstract, New Delhi: Central Secretariat.

(b) Bombay Textile Research Asso. Abstract, 1965-70 — Bi-monthly.

(c) Indian Science Abstract, Delhi: INSDOC, 1965 — Monthly.

(d) ICSSR Research Abstract. N. Delhi : Oriental Longman, 1972 — Quarterly.

(e) Food Technology Abstract. Mysore: Central Food Technological Research Institute, 1966 — Monthly.

(C) REPROGRAPHY

It is a modern technology which can prepare duplicate copy of a document. It is called Xeroxgraphy, or photocopy. Library can provide a photocopy of any document of the library to research scholars, students and other readers.

According to Encyclopedia of Librarianship — photocopy or other technique to prepare duplicate copy of document is called reprography.

This system has been proved very useful and checks of theft or page cutting in the library.

It is beneficial because:

(a) It helps in printing duplicate copy.

(b) Any number of photocopies can be prepared.

(c) It is time saving.

(d) Reader may consult the reading material at house.

(e) It is cheaper than type copy.

(f) It helps in Inter-library borrowing

(D) TRANSLATION SERVICE

Researches are going on in every subject and in every country. These researches or articles are published in many languages. These are mostly in science and technology and required for consultation by the scientists of other countries. Being published in other language or the language of the other countries, there is a need of translation in the regional language or the language of the researcher who wants to consult it. More than 2 lakhs articles and reports are published every year in the world, out of which 50% are in English, 20% in German language, 15% in French language, 10% in Russian language.

Translation service solves this problem of language barrier. Now any scientist or researcher of one country can consult the literature of other country by getting the facilities of translation. Such facilities are provided by the documentation centres, information centres and by computer also.

(E) COMPUTER

It is a boon to modern era. It is a mechanism and process of solving all problems at home or office, library or institution, business or industry. We can call it an electronic mind. It solves all such problems which cannot be solved even after spending much labour and money. Developed countries adopted computers many years before and developed it to higher level to work on big projects. Libraries have also adopted it throughout the world and working for accounting, indexing, abstracting, bibliographical control and information retrieval. There are few languages for computer working and to prepare a programme, *i.e.* ALGOL, FORTRAN, COBOL, PL/1 and PL/2.

(F) IMPORTANT INFORMATION CENTRES

There are many institutions and libraries at National and International level, which are serving the community and providing information. These have developed data bank and also established data centres. Informations are selected, accessed and retrieved. Libraries provide current informations.

Important institutions and libraries are as under:

1. IISAST (International Information System for Agriculture Science and Technology)
2. ASLIB (Association of Special Libraries and Information Bureau)
3. UNESCO (United Nations Educational Scientific and Cultural Organization)
4. International Nuclear Information Centre
5. FID (Federation International Documentation)
6. VINITI (All Union Institute of Scientific and Technical Information)

7. MEDLARS (Medical Literature Analysis and Retrieval System)
8. ICSU (International Council for Scientific Union)
9. IFLA (International Federation of Library Association)

Indian Institutions

1. NISCAIR (National Institute of Science Communication and Information Research), New Delhi — (Previously known as INSDOC)
2. DESIDOC (Defence Science Information and Documentation Centre), New Delhi
3. Social Science Documentation Centre
4. DRTC (Documentation Research and Training Centre)
5. IASLIC (Indian Association of Special Libraries and Information Centres).

Reference Questions and their Types

10

Ordinarily, reference service can be divided into two categories:

(a) Direct

(b) Indirect

Direct reference service means personal assistance which could help the readers to search his information. Reference librarian provides guidance and consultation direct to the readers and also direct him to consult the reference books. We call such service direct reference service.

Indirect reference service means the selection of important reference tools, obtain them through purchase or through inter library loan service and provide reference service to the readers. Bibliographies and their preparation and demand of the readers is also indirect reference service. In short, direct reference service is personal service through reference counter or reference tools, while indirect reference service is through reference tools with guidance and consultation.

Readers generally consult Reference librarians. Readers may be of different types, nature, requirements. They put their problems before the librarian and are served immediately in person or through reference tools.

(A) REFERENCE QUESTIONS

Reference questions or queries have no definitions. Generally, when reader enters the library he comes with some object and needs some information in physical form or personally with the librarian. Reader always comes in the library either to collect the information or to trace the information. He requests the librarian or the library staff for help or guidance which is responded by the librarian or through reference books. Queries may be answered by the librarian or through the reading material, *i.e.* books, periodicals or librarians knowledge and intelligentsia.

Some questions may be formal "Which staff available", "Where is the reference section", "What are the rules of lending", "Whether documents may be taken from the library", etc. Such questions are not reference queries but general questions.

According to Margarat Hutchins — Reference questions means such questions which need specific information. Such information can be traced in books, periodicals and reference books. Some questions are not answered because of non-availability of the reference tools in a library.

(B) KINDS OF REFERENCE QUESTIONS

Many librarians have arranged reference queries in many categories, such as:

(a) Directional questions

(b) Ready reference questions

(c) Specific search questions

(d) Research questions

(a) Directional Questions

These are general questions which can be answered within no time under short range reference service. Reference librarian provides answers of such questions with his intelligentsia or with the help of reference sources.

For example:

(1) Where are catalogues kept?

(2) What is the arrangement of catalogue?

(3) Where are Encyclopedia and bibliographies arranged?

(4) Whether Encyclopedia Britannica is available in the library?

(b) Ready Reference Questions

There are questions which can be answered as information is already available in reference books. Such questions can be answered immediately within a time period of 1 minute to 5 minutes. For example:

(1) What is the length of Ganga river?

(2) Who is the author of Godan?

(3) What is the name of the Ambassador of India in America?

(c) Specific Search Questions

There are a few specific questions which are answered with the help of reference sources. Such answers take some more time. This category includes serious questions. If an author is writing a book or doing research on some problem or subject, he needs information relating to his project. For example:

(1) Preparation of radio talk.

(2) Preparation for debate topic.

(3) Essay on contribution of Prem Chand.

(4) Article on DBMS.

All such questions require references.

(d) Research Questions

Research scholars put up many questions before the Reference librarian. Reference librarian arranges all questions in a sequence and searches their answers. He makes the information available in the campus or outside the campus. In this way Reference librarian becomes a friend of researcher and assists him in his problems. He manages and prepares bibliographies, indexes, abstracts, etc. arranging the reference sources, and searches the information against the questions. There are various types of questions.

For example:

(1) Why men have more criminal behaviour than women?

(2) Why election of American President is fought directly?

Such questions take more time and hence long range reference service is provided.

(e) Kinds of Reference Questions

(1) Language questions
(2) Background questions
(3) Trend questions
(4) Questions about persons
(5) Questions about places
(6) Questions about organizations
(7) Question about printing material
(8) Question about facts and current events

(1) Language questions

Such questions include defining words, meaning of words of different languages, pronunciation, meaning of technical words, short forms of words, synonyms, meaning of specific words of regional language, proverbs, etc. In this way all word meanings and their forms come under this category.

(2) Background questions

There are many questions put up or asked by the readers which need study of the background of the question. Such questions can be answered with the help of Encyclopedias. All background informations like origin, history, geographical, environment and other informations are given in Encyclopedias. Such questions come under this category.

(3) Trend questions

There is always a trend of development, working, activities and procedures in a subject study. Such questions pertaining to such informations are known as trend questions. Such questions are generally related to modern behaviour, subject development, knowledge development, new events, industries, science, art, history and political science. Such questions may be answered by annuals, yearbooks and directories, etc.

(4) Questions about persons

Readers sometimes needs information about the life or death of a person and his whereabouts and reasons for which he is famous or contributions he has made. Such questions are related to birth date, death date, place, family, education, and social status. Such questions may be answered with the help of biographies and autobiographies.

(5) **Questions about places**

Many questions asked or enquired by the readers belong to local, regional, state and country or the world area, which means geographical places. Such questions may be replied with the help of Atlas, globe and subject atlases. Moreover, such questions may be responded by directories.

(6) **Questions about printed materials**

There are many queries of the readers faced by Reference librarians which are related to published literature on subjects, valuable books, literature published in a country, bibliographical detail of a book/document, person, etc., details of authentic and standard books. Such questions may be replied with the help of national bibliographies, subject bibliographies, publishers and printers bibliographies.

(7) **Questions about facts and current events** – Some readers ask or enquire about such information which is important at the end of the year. Such information is related to events, accidents, new discoveries, statistics, etc. These questions may be answered with the help of yearbooks, gazetteers, statistical yearbook, etc.

(f) Related Sources

(1) *Random House Dictionary of English Language*, edited by Jess Stein. N. York: Random House, 1966.

(2) *The Oxford English Dictionary*, Oxford. Clarendon Press, 1933.

(3) *Websters Third New International Dictionary of English Language*. Springfield: Narsachussets, 1961.

(4) *Roget's International Thesaurus*. New York: Crowell, 1977.

(5) *Comprehensive English Hindi Dictionary of Government and Educational Words and Phrases.*

Comp. by Dr. Raghuvira and Others. New Delhi: International Academy of Indian Culture, 1966.

(6) *Comprehensive English-Hindi Dictionary*. By Hardev Bahri. Varanasi: Jyanmandal, 1962. 2 vols.

(7) *Bhargava's Standard Illustrated Dictionary of English Languages*. Anglo-Hindi Ed. by R.C. Pathak. Varanasi: Bhargava Book Depot, 1974.

(8) *हिंदी शब्दसागर.* संपा. श्यामसुंदर. वाराणसी: नागरी प्रचारिणी सभा।

(9) *French-English Dictionary of Science and Technology* by Louis Devies. New York: McGraw Hill, 1976.

(10) *Comprehensive Glossary of Technical Terms in Science*. New Delhi: Commission for Scientific and Technical terminology. Ministry of Education & Soc. Sc., 1973. 3 vols.

(11) *ALA Glossary of Library Terms with a Selection of Terms in Related Fields*. By E.M. Thompson. Chicago: American Library Association.

(12) *Websters new Dictionary of Synonyms*. Springfield: Massachusetts: G. & C. Meeriam.

(g) Some Selected Questions

(1) Give meaning of following words in Hindi with sources. Contact, Bail, Estate, Migration.

(2) Write English words of the following with sources. पक्षपात, परिशिष्ट, भ्रष्टाचार, राजद्रोह।

(3) Meaning of following terms — sources
  (i) Chrimen Falsi ....
  (ii) Culpa levis ....

(4) Origin of word 'Bibliography ....

(5) Full form of following abbreviations
RSVP, UNESCO, IFLA
Source: ....

(h) Questions Related to Encyclopedia — Sources

Name the source of the following:

(1) History of Science.

(2) Inventor of Radio.
(3) Date of Independence of Fiji.
(4) Importance of Vitamin B and C.
(5) Characteristics of Hindu religion.
(6) Description of "Wooden house of troys".
(7) Information about 'Indian Honey'.
(8) Information about Second World War.
(9) Manipur dance.
(10) Who were first to manufacturing paper.

(i) Questions Related to Yearbook — Sources

Name the source of the following:

(1) Details of social and educational development of last year.
(2) Place of I.I.Ts in India.
(3) Important International events of last year.
(4) Who was awarded Mangla Prasad Award last year?
(5) How many workers are engaged in Jute Industry in India?
(6) How many languages and dialects are spoken in India?

(j) Questions Related to Geographical — Sources

Name the source of the following:

(1) Importance of Ajanta, Ellora, Chitrakoot and Kaushambi from geography point of view.
(2) Area of Punjab.
(3) Name the historical monuments of Delhi.
(4) Distance between Delhi and London.
(5) Length of Ganga river.
(6) Area and population of Indonesia.
(7) List of monuments of Agra.
(8) Main tourist attractions of Maharashtra.
(9) Climate of Goa.

(10) Heights of Alps.
(11) Old name of Thailand.
(12) Total mileage of roads in India.
(13) Gold deposits in India.
(14) Where is Ghana.
(15) Capital of Nigeria.

(k) Biographical Questions — Sources

Name the source of the following:

(1) Date of birth and death of Ishwar Chander Vidyasagar and Balgangadhar Tilak.
(2) Date of death of Pt. Jawahar Lal Nehru and Smt. Indira Gandhi.
(3) Biographical sketch of Dr. H.J. Bhabha.
(4) Biographical sketch of an Indian Librarian.
(5) Date of birth of John Guttenberg.
(6) Date of birth of Morarji Desai.
(7) Period of Rajiv Gandhi.
(8) What is the real name of Joseph Conrad.

(l) Questions Relating to Directory — Sources

Name the source of the following:

(1) Scientific Institutions of Great Britain.
(2) Name of Commercial Counsel of India in U.S.A.
(3) Name of Vice Chancellor of Madras University.
(4) Total number of Deemed Universities in India.
(5) Total number of Universities in Great Britain.
(6) Scholarships in higher education in U.K.
(7) Year of Foundation of Royal Society, London.
(8) Reference of FID.
(9) When was Bhabha Atomic Research Centre founded.
(10) Services provided by NISCAIR and ICSSR.

(m) Questions Relating to Bibliographies — Sources

Name the source of the following:

(11) Total number of books published in India in 1980.

(12) Total number of books on Physics published in India in 1980.

(13) Bibliography on Adult Education.

(14) Official publications issued by Ministry of Education.

(15) Books on and by Mahatma Gandhi.

(n) Other Selected Questions — Sources

Name the sources for searching the following questions:

(16) Details of Census of India 2001.

(17) Total population of Australia.

(18) Per capita income in India.

(19) Total area, population of Ahmedabad.

(20) Birth rate statistics in Rajasthan in 1984-85.

(21) Area and population of Madhya Pradesh.

(22) Sugar industries in Maharashtra.

(23) Addresses of publishers in U.S.A.

(24) Currency of Syria.

(25) Exchange rate of dollars and pounds.

(26) Trade agreements of India with Japan.

(27) Recent political events in India.

(28) Brief summary of Swkaria Commission Report.

(29) Average yield of principal crops in India.

PART – II
REFERENCE SOURCES

Evaluation of Reference Sources

11

(1) AUTHORITY

While evaluating a yearbook, the dates and statistics given in yearbook should be considered on the basis of their facts. Publisher should have a famous name and fame in the publishing field. Yearbooks published by the organization of an encyclopedia, are always important and more reliable. All information given should refer the basic source of information.

For example – Two separate yearbooks have given the length of Nil River. One yearbook has mentioned the length. While the other yearbook has given the length of the 'Nile River' with a reference of Encyclopedia Britannica with its page number. It means the information given in second-yearbook is more authentic and reliable.

(2) ARRANGEMENT

There should be an index in a yearbook. Index should be clear and fact-finding and there should be cross reference entries. Index is not similar in all indexes. It differs because of different techniques and procedures adopted by the editors and compilers. There is a mention of detailed contents. Yearbook arrangements are generally alphabetical but it is based on subjects.

(3) PERIOD COVERED

It is the aim of the yearbook to provide details of statistics and events of the year. Publication period is generally certain, comprehensively yearly.

(4) BIBLIOGRAPHY

There is necessarily a bibliography in a yearbook. It is given in the end of yearbook whether it is Business yearbook,

Encyclopedia yearbook, research yearbook. Bibliography has detailed account of the documents consulted, selected or referred.

(A) YEARBOOKS

In the present scientific age, events, researches and activities occur everyday and such informations should be made known to the readers by the librarian. Readers generally demand the current informations. All such informations are published in yearbooks. It highlights the new informations about inventions, events, research projects material and guidance.

(a) Special Features of Yearbooks

(a) It is published once in a year and in one or two or more volumes. If there are monthly or half-yearly or other frequence parts, they are published yearly as comprehensive volumes and made available.

(b) It includes all current informations and research material.

(c) It is also published as yearly supplement of an encyclopedia.

(d) It mentions important dates, statistics, notes, present positions, developments and other details. It may be known as short form of encyclopedia.

(e) It includes business news and informations, daily reports of researches, national problems of one year.

(f) It provides up-to-date informations.

(g) It is limited to a period of one year.

(b) Scope

It may be divided in two parts:

(a) General

(b) Special

(a) **General** – All general informations like encyclopedia are given in a yearbook. Informations related to special activities and subject are given with subject and activities limitations.

(b) Special – Special yearbook is based on special business and subject in a special period. Its scope is specific and its informations are limited to one subject or more than one subject.

1. Main Yearbooks

(1) *American Annual.* New York: American Division, Grolier Corp. Inc., 1923.

(2) *Annual Register of World Events.* London: Languages, 1971.

(3) *Britannica Books of the Year.* Chicago: Encyclopedia Britannica Inc., 1938.

(4) *Collier's Encyclopedia Yearbook.* New York: Crowell Collier – Macmillan Pub. Cr., 1950.

(5) *Country and City Data Book.* Washintgon: Govt. Printers Office, 1962.

(6) *Demographic Yearbook*, New York: Deptt. of Economics and Social Affairs, United States, 1968.

(7) *Commonwealth Yearbook*. London: Newman, 1959.

(8) *Europa Yearbook*. London: Europa Publications. 2 Vols.

(9) *International Yearbook and Statesman's Who's Who.* London: Barkers Peerage, 1953.

(10) *International Statistical Yearbook of Large Towns.* Hague: International Statistical Institute, 1962.

(11) *Municipal Yearbook*. Chicago: International City, 1934 –

(12) *New International Yearbook.* The compendium of world progress. New York: Lunk & Wagan, 1932.

(13) *Statistical Abstract of the United States.* Washington: Govt. Printers Office, 1979.

(14) *Statesman Yearbook, Statistical and Historical Annual of States of the World*. London: Macmillan, 1864.

(15) *The Book of Knowledge*. Annual. N. York: Grolier Society.

(16) *The Story of Our Time: Encyclopedia Yearbook*. New York: Grower Society, 1947.

(17) *World Book Encyclopedia*. Year Book. Chicago: Field Enterprises Education Corp., 1922.

(18) *World Topics*. Quarterly. Chicago: United Educators, 1951.

(19) *Yearbook of Agriculture*. Washington: Govt. Printers Office, 1895.

(20) *Yearbook of Science & Technology*. New York: McGrow Hills, 1962.

(21) *Yearbook of Human Rights*. New York: United Nations, 1968.

Indian Yearbooks

(1) *Annual Current Informations*. New Delhi: Bookhive, 1969.

(2) *Basiki* (Hindi). New Delhi: Hindustan Samachar, 1966.

(3) *Bharat: Barsik Sandarbh Granth* (Hindi). New Delhi: Prakashan Vibhag, 1959.

(4) *Current Affairs. India Pakistan: A Yearbook and A Book of General Knowledge*. Calcutta: A Mukharjee, 1949.

(5) *Facts about India*. New Delhi: Publication Division, 1952.

(6) *Hindustan Yearbook*. Calcutta: M.C. Sarkar, 942-71.

(7) *Indian Cotton Textile Industry*. Annual. Bombay: M.P. Gandhi, 1954.

(8) *Indian Economic Yearbook*. Allahabad: Kitab Mahal, 1957.

(9) *India: a Reference Annual*. New Delhi: Ministry of Information & Broadcasting, 1953.

(10) *Nalanda Yearbook and Who's Who in India and Pakistan*. Calcutta: Nalanda Press, 1962.

(11) *Suneja Banking Yearbook and Who's Who*. New Delhi: 1969.

(12) *Times of India Directory and Yearbook including Who's Who*. Bombay: Benett Colman, 1915.

(13) *Writers and Artist yearbook*. Random Adam & Charles, 1967.

2. Some Important Yearbooks

(a) *Times of India directory and yearbook*

It is a general Reference yearbook, which provides variety of informations. Times of India, Bombay started its publication in 1947. It was published under the heading 'Indian Yearbook' from 1947 and 'India and Pakistan yearbook and who's who, from 1948 & 1951'. Now it is published as Times of India Directory and Yearbook.

It includes following details about:

(1) India
(2) Nature
(3) Natural resources
(4) Constitution
(5) Population
(6) Industry and business
(7) Vidhan Sabha and Lok Sabha
(8) New subjects
(9) Who, what and why
(10) Industrial organizations
(11) Life sketch of important personalities

(b) ***Europa yearbook***

(London: Eurapa Pub., 1959)

It is an important yearbook. It is published in two volumes and covers the informations of the whole world. Two volumes have following informations:

(1) First volume – International Organization, Europe, etc.
(2) Second Volume – Africa, America, Asia, Australia.

(c) ***India: A reference annual***

(New Delhi: Research and Reference Division, Ministry of Information and Broadcasting, Govt. of India, 1953).

It is a Government publication published annually. It is continuously published since 1953. It mentions all informations relating to National Life of Indians on all aspects. Informations given in this document are reliable. It includes informations relating to:

(1) Indian climate
(2) Geographical informations
(3) National Flag
(4) Government activities and achievements
(5) Finance
(6) Defence
(7) Education
(8) Scientific Researches
(9) Planning
(10) Industries
(11) Trade
(12) Transport
(13) National Awards
(14) Sahitya Academic awards.

There is an index given at the end of this reference book. It is an important reference book for informations relating to government.

(d) ***Statesman's yearbook***

(London: Macmillan, 1964, Annual)

It is an international annual yearbook, which includes all informations, events, developments, statistical data of events that took place in the year. Informations are supposed to be reliable and authentic.

Statesman's Yearbook is divided in 4 parts:

(1) First Part – Information regarding United Nations, UNESCO, UNICEF and other related organizations and other international organizations, their establishment, activities, organization, publications, etc.
(2) Second Part – Commonwealth countries

(3) Third Part – U.S.A. and related organizations

(4) Fourth Part – Other Countries of the world.

All countries are arranged alphabetically and their informations are given under the following headings:

(1) History
(2) Contribution
(3) Administration
(4) Area
(5) Population
(6) Education
(7) Health
(8) Finance
(9) Defence
(10) Planning
(11) Agriculture
(12) Business and Industries
(13) Trade
(14) Production
(15) Labour and Employment
(16) Transportation
(17) Communication
(18) Foreign relations.

It is an important reference source widely consulted.

INDIA: A Reference Annual

***INDIA 2002: A Reference Annual*, 1953, New Delhi, Publication Division,** Ministry of Information and Broadcasting, Government of India, 2003.

Introduction

India 2002 is a very important source. Information and data related to India are being published in this source since 1953. There is detailed information given in 'India, a Reference Annual', which is very useful for all types of users. Collection of information is done with the help of Central Ministry, Department and State Governments.

Authority

(a) Government of India, Ministry of Information and Broadcasting, Publication Division, Patiala House, New Delhi.

(b) Compiled and edited by Research, Reference and Training Division.

Scope – In this yearbook information of India, Indian personalities, all important subjects, statistics and data are included. For example —

Geographical Introduction

(1) Land and the people

Political Detail

(2) National symbols

(3) The polity

(4) Defence

Educational Information

(5) Education

(6) Cultural Activities

Science

(7) Scientific and Technological development

Environment and Family Welfare

(8) Environment

(9) Health and family welfare

(10) Welfare

(11) Mass communication

Economics

(12) Basic economic data

(13) Finance

(14) Planning

Agricultural Information

(15) Agriculture

(16) Water Resources

(17) Rural Development
(18) Food and civil supplies
(19) Energy

Commerce

(20) Industry
(21) Commerce
(22) Transport
(23) Communication
(24) Labour

Social Structure

(25) Housing
(26) Justice and Law
(27) Youth Affairs and Sports

Indian History

(28) India and the world
(29) States and Union territories
(30) Diary of National events for the year
(31) General Information

Along with general information following informations are included in it such as:

Executives

(i) President of India
(ii) Vice-President of India
(iii) Prime Minister of India
(iv) Chief Justice of India
(v) Chief Election Commissioner of India

Awards

(vi) Civilian Award
(vii) Recipients of Bharat Ratna
(viii) Civilian awards conferred
(ix) Sangeet Natak Academy Award

(x) Sahitya Academi Award
(xi) Nobel Laureates

Defence

(xii) Commanders-in-Chief
(xiii) Chief of Army Staff
(xiv) Chief of Naval Staff
(xv) Chief of Air Staff
(xvi) Winners of Param Vir Chakra
(xvii) Gallantry Awards
(xviii) National Highways and their length

Important trains

(xix) Important trains

Physical features

(xx) Height of some important Indian Mountain Peaks
(xxi) Length of some important Indian Rivers

Constitution

(xxii) Amendments to the Constitution

Appendices

(i) Government of India
(ii) Members of Parliament

INDEX

Specific Information

Key to numeration:

1 lakh	=	One hundred thousand
10 lakhs	=	One million
1 crore	=	Ten million
100 crores	=	One billion

Treatment – Subject are presented in brief form and in easy language.

In the beginning of this book, information about land of India and persons related to the land are given under the heading "Land and People" which is the first chapter of this book. In this chapter first heading is "Physical Background" which is given in bold letters. Matter is arranged as follows:

1. Land and the People

Physical background

Physical features
Geological structure
Rivers
Climate
Flora
Fauna

Demographic background

Census
Population
Population density
Sex ratio
Literacy

Note: In this reference source there is mention from starting page National Flag and National Emblem given as coloured pictures.

2. National Symbol

National Flag
National Emblem
National Anthem
National Song
National Calendar
National Animal
National Bird
National Flower

3. The Polity

The Union and its territories

Citizenship
Fundamental Rights
Fundamental Duties
Directive Principles of State Policy

The Union

Executive
Fundamental Right
Rajya Sabha & Lok Sabha
Qualification for membership of Parliament
Function and powers of Parliament
Parliamentary Committees
Leaders of Opposition in Parliament
Government Business in Parliament
Consultative Committee

Administrative Set up

Ministries / Departments of Government

Public Services

All India Services, Central Secretariat Services
Union Public Service Commission, Staff Selection Commission

Official Language

Training Committees/Samiti
Award Scheme, Publications, Comptroller and Auditor General

Administrative Reforms and Public Grievances

Administrative Tribunals.

The States

Executive Governor
Council of Ministers
Legislature, Legislative Council
Legislative Assembly, powers and functions
Reservation of bills, control over executives

Union Territories

Local Government

Municipalities
Panchayats

Selection Commission

Registration of Political Parties

Reservation of Seats

Electronic Voting Machines, General Elections

Arrangement

(1) In this book arrangement of information is done under subject, sub-subject and sub-sub-subject. For example:

5 – Education

5a – Elementary Education

5b – Secondary Education

5c – University and Higher Education

5d – Education for specific persons

5d (i) – Education for scheduled castes and scheduled tribes

5d (ii) – Education for women's equality

(2) At the end of this book index is given in which information is arranged alphabetically:

A

Act

Administrative Reforms and Public Grievances

Aged, Apprentices

Special Features

In this reference book data is presented through the medium of charts, tables graphs, maps. For example:

(i) The Polity
Table 3.1: Lok Sabha and its Speakers from time to time.

(ii) Health and Family Welfare
Graph: Acceptors of family welfare methods

Physical Format

1. Its binding is of both types, *i.e.* paperback and hardboard.
2. Its printing is clear and special informations are given in bold letters.
3. Paper used in this book is of good quality.

Conclusion

1. In this yearbook all important events and information related to India are included. Hence it is a useful reference source for all type of readers.
2. Its data and information are more reliable as it is published by Government of India.
3. It is an important informative reference tool through which all the activities occurring in India can be known.

(e) *Census of India – 2001*

Registrar General and Census Commissioner, India.

Introduction

Census of India is an important reference source of India. It is a medium through which real form of census can be viewed. This census report not only shows decrease or increase in population but provides various information of people of a country in the form of data.

In every field such statistical information is necessary. The earliest references of use of census in India can be traced back to the Mauryan period in Kautilya's "Arthshastra" (321-296 BC) and later during the Mughal period in "Aain-e-Akbari".

A systematic modern population census in its present scientific form was conducted non-synchronously between 1865 and 1872 in different parts of the country. India's first census on all India basis was carried out in 1881. From this time census is continued without any failure and census survey is conducted, after every 10 years. The census of India 2001 is the 14th census in this continuous series as reckoned from 1872 and the 6th since independence.

Authority

1. This census was first organized by Jayant Kumar Bantnia of the Indian Administrative Service, Registrar General and Census Commissioner, India.

2. Its publication is done by Controller of Publications, New Delhi.

Scope

1. The census report contains the details of population of Nation, Tehsil, District and other geographical units of nation and on the basis of this the statistics of other data is tabled.
2. Following types of information is included:
   (a) Figure at a glance
   (b) Provisional population totals
   (c) Size growth rate and distribution of population
   (d) Population projection
   (e) Density of population
   (f) Sex composition of population
   (g) State of literacy.
3. In Annexure of 'Census of India' list of directors of census operation, composition, of technical advisory committee for census of India 2001, house list schedule, household schedule, glimpses of women's work, national map of rural and ubran areas are included.

Treatment

1. In each chapter information is arranged under statements, under which tables, maps and diagrams are included:

   Statement 1: Population of selected countries

   Statement 2: Population and its growth, India 1901-2001
2. Most information is given in statistical data.
3. Information regarding child population, literate population, workers, non-workers is collected and compiled.

Special Features

1. Three new states Jharkhand, Chhattisgarh, Uttranchal and a large number of new districts are included.

2. Colourful tables, charts, maps and diagrams are given to classify data in which following informations are included. For example:

Table 1: Distribution of population, sex ratio, density and decadal growth rate of population 2001.

Table 2: Total population, child population, in the age group 0-6, literates, literacy rate by sex 2001.

Table 3: Percentage, decadal variation in population: 1901-11 to 1991-2001.

Table 4: States and Union Territories arranged in descending order of growth rate of population: 1961-71 to 1991-2001.

Table 5: Projected and actual population of India, States and Union territories 1971, 1981 and 1991.

Maps

Map 1: Administrative Division 2001.

Map 2: New Districts 1991-2001.

Map 3: New States 1991-2001.

Map 4: Percentage decadal growth of population, 1991-2001.

List of Diagrams

Figure 1: India in world population.

Figure 2: Growth rate of population in India and selected countries (Average annual exponential growth rate 1991-2001).

Figure 3: Decadal growth of population, India 1901-2001.

3. Footnotes are given where necessary. For example: See Note 1 below 'Figures at a glance'.

4. At various places name of sources are also given:

   (a) Population figure for India as per Census 2001.

   (b) Population figure of USA and Japan as per Census 2000.

(c) Other figures are based on world population prospectus, 1998 Revision (Vol. 11) United Nations.

5. Bold letters are also used.
6. Separate colourful maps are enclosed, *e.g.*

(a) India administrative division 2001.

(b) India new districts 1991-2001.

Arrangement

1. Information is arranged chapterwise
2. In Census of India 2001, States/Union territories are arranged in alphabetical order.

Physical Format

1. Information is arranged chapterwise.
2. In Census of India 2001, States/Union Territories are arranged alphabetically.
3. Its binding is paperback.
4. Its printing is clear.
5. Information is arranged in the form of data.

Merits

1. It is government publication so information given in it is authentic and based on facts.
2. Information related to population of country can be obtained from it.
3. The descriptive and statistical report given in it is very useful.
4. Tables, diagrams, graphs, etc. given in it make the search of information easy.
5. Data given in it is not only useful in India only but for the whole world.
6. Statistics of population of state, district, village and all other geographical units has been given and on the basis of these statistics, statistical study of social, educational, economical, cultural, scientific, languages information is given.

Demerits

1. Census is carried out after every 10 years, so latest data is not available in it all the time.
2. The statistical data given in it such as population gets obsolete with time.
3. Index is not given whereas index of words indicating place, subject and terms is necessary.
4. Through census we cannot know detailed information of the nation.

Conclusion: Census of India is not only useful for India but for whole world. It is an important information source through which we can study statistical data related to census of India.

(B) DIRECTORY

It is a list of persons or organisations, systematically arranged, usually in alphabetic or classified order, giving address, applications, etc. for individuals, and addresses, officers, functions and similar data for organisation.

There are several national and international institutions relating to education, commercial business, public institutions, social, economic and cultural institutions. These institutions are serving the society for their lifestyle, employment, production, profession, vocational, and other day-to-day activities in the welfare of man to provide necessary knowledge and facilities. Readers and the common man needs all informations related to such institutions, such as their names, addresses, location, work and activities, nature, field of work and research and their branches.

Directories are helpful in many fields. Reference librarian takes necessary help of directories to answer the queries of the readers. Directory as clear from its name, works for direction. There are directions in directories which are useful for research work and general informations. Such directions may be related to persons, groups of persons, branches, clubs, hotels, etc. Directories have an index of persons and institutions.

According to ALA Glossary, Directory is systematically arranged list of persons and institutions according to their subjects and sequence, in which their names, addresses, activities, offices, officers and their organizational informations are given.

1. Objectives

Though dictionary, encyclopedia, gazetteers, atlas and annuals give directional informations, yet Directory has its special importance. Its objects are as under:

(a) It provides information of addresses, telephone numbers of the institutions.

(b) Full name of the persons or the institutes.

(c) Details of production and working of producers.

(d) Replies of questions put up with 'who'. For example: Who is the President of India? Who is Vice Chancellor of Agra University? Who are the major steel producers in India?

(e) Up to date informations about life sketch of persons.

(f) History and current statistics regarding establishment and directors of institutions.

(g) Business and professional informations of doctors, engineers, contractors, cement producers, transporters, etc.

2. Kinds of Directories

There are 5 kinds of directories:

(a) Local directories

(b) Government directories

(c) Institutional directories

(d) Professional directories

(e) Trade and business directories

(a) Local directories

Local directories are limited to a place or local region.

For example:

(i) Telephone directories
(ii) City directories

(b) Government directories

Directories are prepared and published by Govt. — State, National or their departments.

For example:

(i) Post and telegraph directory

(ii) Air service directory

(iii) Govt. Transport / Road directory

(iv) Train directory

(c) Institutional directories

Directories which are prepared and published by institutions are called Institutional directories.

For example:

(i) University Handbook

(ii) Museum Directory

(iii) Directory of research libraries of India.

(d) Professional directories

Such directories have list and details of professional persons, *i.e.* lawyers, doctors, librarians, businessmen, industrialists and officers.

(e) Trade directories

Such directories mention the list of companies, industries, and private institutions.

For example:

Star directory

Rotary directory

Therefore, directories provide the facts about the persons and institutions of the readers. It has following necessities:

(a) Able editorial which can edit the directory efficiently

(b) Style of writing, directional method

(c) Subject compilation.

Directories have the similar presentation. They differ in area, subject and bibliographical details. Directories need revision from time to time, to make them up to date.

3. Main Directories

(a) *Publisher's World*. N.Y.: R.R. Bowker, 1967.
(b) *International Literary Market Places*. New York: R.R. Bowker, 1967.
(c) *American Library Directory*. New York: Bowker, 1967.
(d) *Directory of International Scientific Organizations*. Paris, Unesco, 1950, 1967, 1978.
(e) *Business Directory*. New York: Free Public Library, 1934.
(f) *Directory of Directories*. London: Business Pub., 1950.
(g) *Trade Directory of the World*. New York: Crooner Pub., 1969.
(h) *London Directory and International Register of Manufacturers*. London: Directory Co., 1967.

4. Indian Directories

(a) *All Indian Telegraphic Address Directory, Baroda*. Indian Export Trade Jrl., 1970.
(b) *All India Telephone Directory*.
(c) *City Telephone Directory*.
(d) *Delhi City Guide and Directory*.
(e) *Teacher's Indian Directory*. Calcutta: Thacker Press, 1971.
(f) *Indian Press*, New Delhi: Pub. Division, 1971.
(g) *Indian Business Directory. Exporters and Importers*. New Delhi: Chamber of Commerce, 1971.
(h) *Times of India Directory and Yearbook*. Bombay: Benmer Colman, 1915.
(i) *Indian Oilseeds Directory*. New Delhi: ICAR, 1963.
(j) *Tea Directory*. Calcutta: Tea Board, 1966.
(k) *Indian Trade Directory*. Bombay: International Trade Centre, 1946.
(l) *Directory of Indian Manufacturers*. Bombay: IIMO, 1968.

5. World of Learning

World of Learning is an important reference tool/source published by Europa Publications, London, it is annual and is published in two volumes.

Introduction

It is a directory and provides information on education on regional, state, national and international level. This reference source gives details of institutions, related persons, institutions, address, name, location, functions, nature and other related informations.

According to ALA Glossary of Library Terms, the 'World of Learning' is sequential list, and detail of institutions and their related persons and authorities in which the persons, working activities and also the name, address, authorities, are given for references.'

'World of Learning' is an international directory, which provides all informations of high education of the world. All higher educational institutions are mentioned with their details.

Authority

(a) It is published by a famous publisher Europa Publications, London.

(b) Its first edition was published in 1947.

(c) It is published in two volumes.

Scope – It covers:

(a) Higher Educational Institutions.

(b) Libraries, faculty, department and list of affiliated institutions along with telephone numbers.

(c) Authorities and the addresses.

(d) 27000 universities, institutions, museums, board of studies, rules for admission etc.

(e) In its first part more than 500 International Educational, scientific, cultural institutions and organizations are given with important informations under specific headings.

(f) There is an index in the end.

Treatment – This reference source has following informations regarding International Institutions and organizations:

(a) Name of institution
(b) Year of establishment
(c) Address
(d) Telephone, website, e-mail
(e) Period of session
(f) Control authority
(g) Medium of institutions
(h) Name of V.C., Registrar, Director, Principal, etc.

Special Features

There is an index at the end of the each volume which is helpful in tracing the information in need. Additional informations are included every year to make it up to date.

Arrangement

This directory is arranged alphabetically according to the names of the states. States are also arranged alphabetically.

Physical Format

It has a hardbound physical format. It is well printed on good quality paper which is used to make it attractive and easily readable.

Merits – This directory provides necessary information about the organizations/institutions of international, national, regional and local level.

Demerits – Even after making efforts to include related informations and make it uptodate, there are few informations left to include.

This reference source is costly and very difficult for the small libraries to buy it.

Conclusion – It is an international directory in which all universities/colleges of the world are included which is helpful to all educational institutions, research scholars and students.

6. University Handbook

It is a publication of Association of Indian Universities, New Delhi.

Introduction

This Handbook is an important source of information in the field of higher education. It gives information of all universities and colleges and other research institutes.

Authority

(a) The Association of Indian Universities publishes this handbook every alternate year.

(b) It is being published since 1927.

Scope

It includes information of 273 universities and national institutes, *i.e.*

(a) Universities
(b) Deemed Universities
(c) Agriculture Universities
(d) Technical Institutions
(e) Medical Institutions
(f) Information Technology Institutions
(g) Law Universities
(h) Universities for Journalism
(i) Open/Distance Education Universities
(j) Nepal and Mauritious Universities are also included in this handbook.
(k) Vocational Institutes – Industrial Training Institutes, Political Institutes, professional bodies.
(l) It has given a list of abbreviations.
(m) There is an index at the end of this handbook.

Treatment

The following informations are included in this handbook:

(a) Name of Administrative Officers, Chancellor, Vice-Chancellor, pro-Vice-Chancellor, Librarian, Faculty members upto the rank of Readers.

(b) Academic year
(c) Admission period
(d) Period of examinations
(e) Hostel facilities
(f) Library facilities
(g) Courses and subject
(h) Name and facilities provided by departments
(i) Number of readers in libraries
(j) Number of students in each course
(k) Name of colleges, principals.

Special Features

It is divided in four parts:

(a) Subject
(b) Degree and Diplomas
(c) Summary of the universities
(d) Informations of universities of Nepal, Mauritius.

Physical Format

(a) It has a hardboard binding.
(b) It has used a good quality of paper for printing.

Merits

(a) It is published in alternate years.
(b) It has given the list of affiliated colleges.
(c) It is an important source of informations.
(d) It is useful for ready reference service.

Demerits

(a) It is published on alternative years.
(b) Matter is not discussed with the help of tables and diagrams.
(c) It is a costly reference source.

Conclusion

It is an important handbook of informations related to higher education. It is very helpful to libraries.

7. Important Directories

(a) *World of Learning*

(London: Europa Publication, 1947). It is an important yearbook. There are many institutions of higher education in all countries, which are required and demanded by the readers in Academic and other libraries. It has two volumes:

First Volume: It mentions the information of more than 400 international educational, scientific and cultural institutions. Other important national institutions are also given along with their details. All these institutions are arranged alphabetically.

Second Volume: Second volume mentions the Index of all educational institutions.

World of learning as clear from its name has given detailed account of Academic, scientific and cultural institutions including:

(a) Higher educational institutes

(b) Universities

(c) Colleges

(d) Museums and art galleries

(e) Research institutions.

The information regarding these institutions includes:

(a) Name of the institute

(b) Address of the institute

(c) Activities.

(C) BIBLIOGRAPHY

Bibliography is a systematic description and history of books, their authorship, printing, publishing, editions. It is a list of books of a particular author, printer or country, or those dealing with any particular theme, the literature or a subject. Bibliography is a study of books as material objects, irrespective of their contents.

A bibliography may include a detailed description of the books themselves and in this sense the bibliographer requires a knowledge not only of the history of typography but also of book-binding and paper-making. A bibliography may be an author bibliography, descriptive bibliography, textual bibliography, analytical bibliography, critical bibliography and bibliography of bibliographies.

A bibliography covers title pages including ornaments and borders, unprint, colophons, implicits and explicits, binding and casting preliminaries, imprints, advertisement, texts and collations, preface and dedication, etc. Collation paragraph has full standard descriptions. Full, short, medium, standard descriptions are accepted as the normal type of entries.

Bibliographies, covering as they do everything which is written or printed, will also cover maps, illustrations, song and gramophone records and thematic catalogue.

Definitions

Aberts – "Bibliography is a science which help in studies."

Ranganathan – "Systematic arrangement of informations is a bibliography."

Coule – "Bibliography is systematic arrangement of books of a subject or subjects."

Humes – "Bibliography is arrangement of writing material."

1. History of Bibliography

In ancient period clay tablets were used and arranged in sequence. Nalanda Vishwavidyalaya also listed their manuscripts.

It was originated from Greek word – 'Biblion + Graphem'. Biblion means 'book' and 'Graphem' means writing. During second century bibliography was known as writing the book. Fanix English dictionary explained in 1761 the bibliography as 'copy of the book'. The bibliography means the creating a book with detail. Greg says bibliography represents the object of the book but it does not represents the subject of the book. He agreed to this point that bibliography mentions the detail of the book. In fact the bibliography concept existed before printing press.

During the 15th century printing press were started. With the advent the printing process, books of many authors were produced in many numbers. This resulted in listing of books along with their details. It was named 'list of books', 'arrangement of books', 'process of writing', book science, etc. During 19th century bibliography was used and people were known with its importance. It was given serious thought. Many bibliographies were prepared. For example — 'detailed bibliography', 'analysed bibliography'. Their arrangements were somehow similar, *i.e.* alphabetical, chronological, subject-wise and geographical. The first bibliography was 'Libre de Scripteniluis acclessiasticis', which was prepared in 1494. It was compiled by Johtan Zithem. The first international fame bibliography was prepared by Conrad Gesner of Zurich in 1545 which was known as 'Biblio Theca Universalis'.

During 1548 John Wale prepared National Bibliography "Illustrium Majoris Brittannial". During 6th century one more effort was made in Germany while a bibliography on trade was prepared.

In fact bibliography age started from 18th century with the bibliography 'Bibliotheca Biliothecarum' which was prepared by Phillips Leweep. He made a few amendments to make the bibliography more useful and effective. In 1726 Cotton Methew prepared a bibliography 'Bibliography of theological and Biblical literature'. "A moderate and revised bibliography, Bibliographic Insuctine" was published by Guh Lowey in 10 volumes in 1763-82. It mentioned full details of the book. It was a famous bibliography of its period.

At later stage author, title and subject bibliographies were published. But bibliography was known as the source of old books as it was normal to print a bibliography in two years time. Lowig House published a bibliography "Referterium Bibliographicum and annum M.D." which was a list of old books.

Other important bibliographies were:

(a) Index to the early printing books in British Museum by Robert Proctors.

(b) Catalogue catalogorum by Theodore Anfrahts, 1891-1901.

(c) Bibliothecal Sanskrita, 1847 by John Gildemeister.

The above bibliographies were small in detail and books were not more in number. Later, bibliographies were published in many countries:

(a) France – 1811 "Bibliographic de la France".

(b) England – 1950 "British National Bibliography".

(c) India – 1958 "Indian National Bibliography".

Many countries started Bibliographical Research Centre like F.I.D. and Bibliographic Society, London, National Library, Calcutta. There are many universities which are publishing their bibliographies.

2. Library Catalogue *vs.* Bibliography

Following points are highlighted while comparing Library Catalogue and Bibliography:

(a) Library catalogue is a list of library books arranged in a systematic way, while bibliography is a list of books not limited to a library or the type of books.

(b) Both are lists of books but library catalogue has some limitations.

(c) Library catalogue is useful to the readers who are members of the library, while bibliography is helpful for all readers of a library or outsiders and research scholars.

(d) Library catalogue can be consulted in a library at any time and books may be taken for use, while books mentioned or listed in bibliography are to be managed, purchased or arranged through inter-library loan.

(e) Library catalogue mentions classification number or any other code number to trace the book in the library, as these numbers indicate the location of the book, while in bibliography no such code number or location number is mentioned.

(f) Library catalogue is prepared according to the standard catalogue code and its rules, while bibliography has no such standard rules.

(g) In a library catalogue a book has many approaches,

i.e. author, title, subject, series, etc. but in bibliography a book will have only one or two approaches.

3. Importance of Bibliography

Bibliography is a connecting factor between library and the book.

User → bibliography → library

(a) Using the library

(b) Acquiring the book

It saves the time of the reader and provides informations in book selection and obtaining the book in library. Bibliographies give many informations which a reader does not know. Reader is not generally aware of the author and title. He presents his difficulties before the reference librarian, who suggests him many readings on the subject with the help of the bibliography. If the book is not available in the library, reference librarian will arrange the book under inter-library loan system. He consults the bibliography and knows the detail of the book and arranges it for the reader.

Bibliography is necessary because of following reasons:

(a) It gives all bibliographical details of a book, *i.e.* author, title, subject, pages, price, edition, illustrations, etc.

(b) Bibliographies are helpful in case the library catalogue fails to guide the readers about the book required and necessary arrangement may be made to obtain the book.

(c) Subject bibliographies provide information of the books on the subject.

(d) Author bibliography helps the reader to trace the book of his choice author. If an author has written four books on different aspects of a subject, for example *Indian Tax System*, *British Banking System*, *Principle of Money*, *Components of Insurance*. All details of these books may be available in Author bibliography under the name of one author.

(e) **Standard of the book** – Many authors have written books on one subject. The standard or the quality of book depends on the status of the author. A good author or publisher generally writes the quality books. On the other hand it is not true that a small publisher is not supposed to publish a quality book. If the book has a good author, whether published by a small publisher, the book will be a quality book. In addition to author diagrams, tables, new editions, illustrations also make the book qualitative.

(f) **Research work** – Researcher always needs new and latest books for his research work. Research work is always qualitative if good books are consulted. Such books may be searched in bibliographies.

4. Functions of Bibliography

There are following functions of a bibliography:

(a) **Preparation of bibliography is an art** – Preparation and presentation of bibliography is a technique in which other factors also contribute. Art represents man, material, nature, economic and social aspects. For example if we want to draw a monkey then the artist will make it like a living element with the help of colours, size, organs, genes, area and the place and will complete with imagination. Similarly bibliography mentions all bibliographical details like author, title, edition, publisher's full address, pages, illustrations, size, colour, binding, paper and printing, etc. It is also like an art. As a small mistake in an art of an artist can deface or deconcept the work of art and make it meaningless or ugly. Similarly any lack of detail can put the reader confused or mistaken and the bibliography will not be effective.

(b) **Bibliography is a science** – Bibliography has its own systems and procedures which is a basis of it. It is prepared under some procedures which is a basis of it. It is prepared by various means, *i.e.* author, title, subject, etc. and principles and procedures are followed.

Its systems are like science formula which does not allow any change. Similarly in a bibliography, the details of a book are represented after a thorough study, rules and regulations. All aspects of a book are considered and represented on scientific basis. Bibliography is prepared with serious considerations of illustrations, sequence of pages, sequence of author, sequence of title, sequence of publisher, sequence of subject, suitable binding, adequate printing etc. Any mistake can disregard the bibliography. Therefore, bibliography is a science which is analysed on scientific basis.

(c) **Location** – Publisher has an important place after the consideration of the name of the book and the author because book collection is incomplete till all procedures are adopted to prepare the bibliography. A book cannot be obtained without the information about the publication. Bibliography mention full details of the publisher.

The other problem is to trace a book of a particular subject. Subject bibliography help to trace a particular book on a subject as it provides a list of all books of one or many subjects. Such bibliography includes manuscripts, periodicals and other media sources.

(d) **Verification** – Generally bibliographies provide reliable informations, *i.e.* author, title, edition, publisher's place, name and year, pages and illustrations. Any of these informations may be obtained from bibliography. It also provides informations about the published books whether historical, social, and economic aspect.

(e) **Selection** – It is the primary duty of the library to collect the best and qualitative books. Good books always help the readers. A good reference librarian is judged by making selection of the books. Bibliography makes the book selection easier. It provides information of all books by one author or books by all authors on the subject. While making book selection all bibliographical details are made available by the bibliography.

5. Important Components of Standard Bibliography

(a) **Completeness** – Bibliography, whether of one subject or many subjects, its collection should be complete in all respects. Reference librarian, while preparing bibliography, should take precautions that all books pertaining to one area and region should cover complete publications. All ancient, medieval and modern books should be included in the bibliography. A wide area should be selected in a bibliography.

(b) **Special informations** – In the modern age when there is a knowledge explosion, it is not a wise step to cover all books of all subjects in a bibliography. On the other hand a bibliography should cover one specific subject or the specific aspect of one subject. Such bibliographies are very beneficial to the researchers.

For example – one bibliography on each aspect of economics, such as money, banking, tax, etc. should be prepared so as to give specific informations of a specific aspects.

(c) **Various categories** – Bibliography is prepared in many forms, such as:

First category

(i) Author
(ii) Title
(iii) Subject
(iv) Publisher

Second category

(i) Analytical bibliography
(ii) Systematic bibliography
(iii) Descriptive bibliography
(iv) Trade bibliography

6. Bibliographical Services

Bibliographical services are very important services. They include three processes:

(a) Preparation

(b) Service

(c) Assimilation.

7. Qualities of Bibliographer

(a) Subject knowledge – Bibliographer should be a qualified and experienced hand as it will help him to deliver his services. Bibliographer should have knowledge of all subjects. This knowledge will be helpful in answering the reader's queries relating to the subject. If a bibliographer has no knowledge of a subject, then he will not understand the query and won't be able to answer properly which will be a loss of energy and time.

For example – If one reader has a query about 'Tax settlement', if the bibliographer has no knowledge of the subject, he will fail to provide services. This query will be covered under 'Public Finance'. Bibliographer may consult bibliography on commerce or finance and serve the reader.

(b) Knowledge of Reference Sources – Bibliographer should have a knowledge of reference sources in addition to subject knowledge. Bibliographer should be aware of all the important authors, titles, publishers and subject bibliographies. He should get himself up to date with all latest publications of the bibliographies, their special features, the details of bibliographies may be found in "Bibliography of Bibliographies":

(i) Index Bibliographics

(ii) F.I.D. list of current specialized abstracting and indexing services.

(iii) Guide to the reference material

(iv) Guide to the reference books

(v) Bibliography of bibliographies.

8. Author Bibliography

(a) **Area** – Author bibliography means the bibliography covering the books of one author or one of the authors. It includes:

(i) Books on one author

(ii) Books by an author

(iii) Books written under joint authorship

(iv) Books written by anonymous, or pseudonym author

(v) Reviews on the books of an author.

(b) **Arrangement** – Author bibliography is arranged alphabetically. It is arranged 'word by word' or 'letter by letter'. All precautions should be taken while arranging authors and publishers. One author may be in any form, *i.e.* poet, artist, cartographer. In such matters the entry should have all details.

9. Main Author Bibliographies

1. Aruin, Max. *International Personal Bibliography, 1800-1943*.
2. Deshpande, P.G. (comp.). *Gandhiana: A Bibliography of Gandhian Literature*. Ahmedabad: Navjiwan Pub. House, 1948.
3. Dharmvir. *Gandhi Bibliography*. Chandigarh: Gandhi Smarak Nidhi, 1967.
4. Ghoshal, Hirendra Nath (comp.). *Ravindra Sahitya Abhinav*. Calcutta: The Compiler, 1961.
5. Kerla, P.N., ed. *Malviyana: A Bibliography of Pandit Madan Mohan Malviya*. Comp. By M.M. Jab and I.B. Singh. Varanasi: Varanasi Hindu Vishwavidyalaya, 1962.
6. Parkes, Alen. *James Joyce: A Bibliography of His Writings*. Boston: F.M. Faxton, 1948.
7. Panjab University Library. *Dr. Zakir Hussain: A Bibliography*. Chandigarh, 1968.
8. Pardesi, Ram Gopal Barua. *Lokhak Kosh*. Agra: Santvan Pub., 1971, Chand 1-2.

9. Sharma, J.S. (comp.). *Jawaharlal Nehru: A Descriptive Bibliography*. Delhi: S. Chand, 1955.
10. Sharma, J.S. (comp.). *Mahatma Gandhi: A Descriptive Bibliography*. Delhi: S. Chand, 1955.

10. Subject Bibliographies

Subject bibliography provides informations of subject books. A list of books on one subject or its group of subjects published is called subject bibliography. There have been few efforts made to publish subject bibliographies which caused many problems to trace the books. Indexes are also consulted to trace the subject books instead of subject bibliographies. Subject bibliographies are limited to a particular area, *i.e.* regional, state, national and international. Other limitation is subject limit, *i.e.* Humanities bibliography, bibliography on Physics.

Subject bibliographies are arranged according to subjects based on scheme of classification. There are three systems to arrange entries in subject bibliography.

(a) Class number, sequence of Author

(b) Chronological (for law)

(c) Subject bibliography includes articles also and use cross reference entries.

Main Subject Bibliographies

1. Balton, H. Carrington. *Select Bibliography of Chemistry*. 1492-1902. Washington: Smithsonian, 1892-1992-1904. 4 vols.
2. *Bibliography of Indian Philosophy*. Madras: Aiyer Research Endowment Committee, 1963.
3. Books on India: *A Select Bibliography of the World*. Jaipur: Rajasthan University, 1967.
4. Boring, Edin G. *List of Books on Psychology*. Cambridge: Harvard Univ. Press.
5. Carnore, H.G.T. *Bibliography of Library Economy*. Chicago: ALA.

6. Dean, *Bashford Bibliography of Fishes*. New York: Am. Museum of National History, 1916. 3 vols.
7. Diehl, K.S. *Religions, Mythologies, Folklore: An Annotated Bibliography*. New York: Scare Crew Press.
8. *International Bibliography of Social Science: Sociology, Pol. Sc. Economics. Authropology*. London: Stonct, 1952. 4 vols.
9. *International Catalogue of Scientific Literature*, 1902-19. 14 Vols. London: Royal Society.
10. Nilon, Charles, ed. *Harward List of Books on Psychology*. Chambridge University Press, 1966. 39 vols.
11. Parke, R.C. *Guide to Literature of Maths and Physics*. New York: McGraw Hill, 1951.
12. Pearl, R.M. *Guide to Geologic Literature*. New York: McGraw Hill, 1951.
13. Roberts, H.L. *Foreign Affairs Bibliography, 1952-1962*. New York: Bowker.
14. Smith, R.C. *Guide to Literature of Zoological Science*. Maunicapalis, Balgers.

Indian Bibliographies

1. *Bibliography of Indian Philosophy*. Madras: Aiyer Research Endowment Committee, 1963.
2. *Books on India: A Select Bibliography of title on India Published in English in all Parts of the World*. Jaipur: Rajasthan University Library, 1967.
3. Dandeedar, R.N., ed. *Vedic Bibliography*. Bombay: Karnataka Pub. House, 1946-61. 2 vols.
4. Fernades, Brag, A. (comp.). *Annual Bibliography on Indian History and Indology*. Bombay: Historical Society, 1933-49. 5 vols.
5. Guba, Partha. *Indian Lib. Science Books*. Calcutta: Information Research Academy, 1970.

6. Gupta, Girraj Pd. Eco. *Investigation in India: A Bibliography of Researches in Commerce & Economics*. Agra: Ram Prasad, 1961.
7. Guru Nanak University. *Religion: A Select Bibliography*. Amritsar: The University, 1970.
8. *Institute of Economic Growth. Social Sc. Bibliography*. 1966. New Delhi: Vikas, 1970.
9. Mehu, C. Chimanlal (comp.). *Bibliography of Stageable Plays in Indian Languages*. New Delhi: Bhartiya Natya Language, 1963.
10. Mores, G.M., ed. *Bibliography on Indological Studies*. Bombay: Economics Press, 1942.
11. Suman Chandra (comp.). *Bibliography of Indian Art and Craft*. New Delhi: Ministry of Home Affairs, 1967.

11. Analytical Bibliographies

Library catalogue gives more emphasis on title of the book, author, publisher so that librarian can approach the maximum number of books as librarian knows the contents of the books. But in analytical bibliography more importance is given to the physical or outer form of a book. The main object of this bibliography is:

(a) Physical features of the books:
   (i) Printing
   (ii) Paper
   (iii) Binding
   (iv) Illustrations.

(b) Difference between the physical features of one book and similar other book.

There are examples when one author copied the book of other author's book and gained profits. Analytical bibliography is a bibliography which gives full details of a book which can be prepared by the experienced and trained librarians.

12. Systematic Bibliographies

Such bibliographies are called general bibliographies. Its object is:

(a) to trace the book;

(b) to guide the location of a book;

(c) to select the book;

(d) its area is specific;

(e) it works as enumerative and classification;

(f) it provides all bibliographical details, their compilation, and serious study of the details of the entries;

(g) Entries are arranged systematically.

Generally all subject bibliographies come under systematic bibliographies: These are used for specific informations and helpful to researchers.

13. Selective Bibliographies

Libraries prepare list of important books, or books mostly on demand. Though such lists are not called bibliographies and also do not come under the preview of the bibliographies. Yet such bibliographies are important and are being used widely. These are useful to the students, traders, youngers, and scientists.

14. Trade Bibliographies

Trade bibliographies are mostly concerned with book trade. These bibliographies help to highlight the details of the books related to the library catalogue. These are very important in books trade. These are published by book traders as publisher's catalogues, catalogues of distributors. Such trade catalogues or bibliographies are useful to select the books for purchasing them in the library. Though all books mentioned in trade bibliography are not current yet they may be available on demand.

Important trade bibliographies are:

(a) American Book Publishing record

(b) Books in Print (US) – Author, title, subject

(c) Bowker's subject guide to books in print
(d) British Books in Print (U.K.)
(e) Cumulative Book Index 1898.
(f) English catalogue of books, 1801.
(g) Publisher's weekly
(h) PTLA (Publishers Trade List Annual)
(i) Whitaker's Cumulative Book lists 1924.

15. Books in Print

Introduction

This bibliographical reference source gives all information about articles published in books and periodicals. It contains details about the name of book, author, editor, title, publisher, translator address and price of book, etc. in arranged form.

Authority

(a) Indian Bibliographical Bureau, Delhi
(b) Compiled and edited by Sher Singh
(c) First edition published in 1967
(d) A bibliography of Indian books published upto Dec. 1980 in English language.

The present bibliography has been divided in to three volumes:

(a) Vol. I – Authors
(b) Vol. II – Titles
(c) Vol. III – Subject Guide.

Scope

(a) Indian books in print are in three volumes and lists approximately 80,000 titles brought out by 2,200 Indian publishers.

(i) *Volume–I is an author Index*

The author index contains entries for each book under the name of personal author, joint author, corporate author, editor, joint editor, compiler, translator, publisher, place of publication, year of publication, pages, price.

(ii) *Volume–II is a title Index*

The title index contains entries for each book under the title, subtitle, author, edition, place of publication, publisher, year of publication, page and price.

1. The information about the book has been given in the following order:

   Class number, author, co-author (if any), editor, compiler, full title, subtitle, edition (if not first), place of publication, publisher, year of publication, number of page, price.

   For example: 020.4

   CORBETT (Edmund Victor)

   Fundamental of Library Organization and Administration: A Practical Guide. New Delhi: Oxford IBH, 1979-x, 291 p., 150.00.

2. In Vol. III subjects are arranged according to 16th edition of DDC with some modification.

   For example: Volume–III — Subject Guide

   Subject Guide
   General Works
   Bibliography
   Library Science
   Essays
   General Societies
   Museums
   Journalism and Newspaper
   Collected works
   Manuscripts and Rare Books
   Philosophy
   Religion
   Social Sciences
   Languages
   Pure Sciences
   Technology and Useful Arts
   Literature
   History, Biography and Travel

3. It is a directory of Indian publishers, the complete address has been given in Volume III.

   Directory of Indian Publishers
   AC Bose,
   86, Girish Chandra Bose Road,
   Nayagaon Lucknow-226001

4. Subject index for subject heading has been given at the end of Volume–III.

   Subject Index
   Accounting
   AFGHANISTAN
   GEOGRAPHY
   HISTORY

(b) With each volume of Indian books in print, a separate key to Abbreviation is given:

abr.	abridged
assn.	ssociation
auth.	author
Bro(s)	brother, brothers,
bk(s)	book, books

Treatment

(a) **In Volume–I (Author)**

(i) Honorific words with the author's name and initial articles, *i.e.* 'a', 'an', 'the' in the beginning of title have been omitted.

(ii) While rendering the name of personal or corporate authors, rule of classified catalogue code have been followed. For example:

Personal	: DUBEY (Shyamji)
Government	: INDIA, INFORMATION AND BROADCASTING (Ministry of —)
Institution	: NATIONAL COUNCIL OF APPLIED ECONOMIC RESEARCH (New Delhi)

Conference : CONGRESSMEN'S CONVENTION FOR SOCIALISM AND SECULARISM (New Delhi) (1979).

(iii) Author, title, edition are arranged according to ALA and other information are arranged according to AACRII

DUBEY (RN),
Economic & Commercial Geography
Ed. 13, Allahabad, Kitab Mahal, 1970
vii, 596 p.

(iv) In case of joint authors the entry regarding the book bears the name of both authors, *e.g.*

KRISHAN KUMAR and GIRJA KUMAR.

(v) If a book is by more than two authors the name of mentioned authors has been used and the word 'etc.' added thereafter

AGASHE (DS), etc.

(vi) An entry is made under title if there is no mention of either author or editor or compiler. The first two letters are given in block letters:

ECONOMIC IMPACT OF Computers in India New Delhi, Marketing and Economic Research Bureau, 1971, 212 p., 15.00.

(vii) Complete bibliographical information relating to each book is given with all added entries. For example:

SRIVASTAVA (Anand P)
Pathology of higher education is some
Challenges before University faculty.
Kanpur, Reprint Publisher, 1979
294 p., 100.00.

(b) **Volume–II (Title Index)**

In Volume-II initial articles 'a' and 'the' have been omitted from the title. For example:

Indian Economy: A descriptive analysis
KPM Sundharam. Ed. 16, New Delhi.
R Chand, 1980, xi, 500 p., 20.00.

(c) **Volume–III (Subject Guide)**

(i) The rendering of names of authors have been done according to Ranganathan's classified catalogue code:

Personal	:	BETEILLE (Andre)
Institution	:	NATIONAL COUNCIL OF APPLIED ECONOMIC RESEARCH (New Delhi)

(ii) Feature headings have been provided along with Dewey numbers:

GENERAL WORKS

001	General Knowledge
010	Bibliography
010.78	Documentation
012	Bibliographies, Individual Authors
015	National Biographies
015.54	India
016	Bibliographies Subject
016.05	Periodicals
016.019	Manuscripts
016.15072	Experimental Psychology

(iii) Where there are two or more works by the same author under a specific subject, the name of the author is not repeated.

(iv) Where number and feature headings are not provided in the Dewey Decimal Classification and the subjects are of Indian or recent origin, new suitable number for such subject have been given. For example:

Public Sector	338.74
Private Sector	338.73
National Integration	320.1580954

Arrangement

Volume–I

(a) Volume-I is an author index in which arrangement given by the author is alphabetical. For example:

AACHEN/BOCHUM-OSMANIA COOPERATION SCHEME SYMPOSIUM ON INDIA YESTERDAY AND TOMORROW (Nyder) Economic & Social Aspects of Indian Development Bombay, Shakuntla Pub. House, 80.00.

(b) Different books by one author are arranged alphabetically:

(i) ABBAS (Khwaja Ahmad)
Barrister at Law, New Delhi, Orient Paperback 1977. 137 p., 5.00.

(ii) Black Sun and Other Stories, Bombay, Jaico. 1963. 114 p., 1.50.

Volume–II

It is a title index where entries are arranged alphabetically.

Blood and Stones: Khwaja Ahmad Abbas.
New Delhi, Hind Kitab, 1949. 48 p., 1.00.

Volume–III

(a) This volume is arranged according to classified alphabetic catalogue:

001 **General Knowledge**
ACKERMANN (Robert)
Theories of Knowledge

016.05 **Periodicals**
BC ROY MEMORIAL LIBRARY
(Calcutta)
Catalogue of Serials

(b) Sub index of Volume–III is also alphabetically arranged and necessary references about any particular subject, state and country are also given and arranged in alphabetical order:

INDIA
ANCIENT INDIA
ASSAM

(c) In Volume–III directory of publishers is also arranged alphabetically:

AH Wheeler
AH Wheeler & Co. Pvt. Ltd.,
15, Elgin Road, Allahabad-211007
AICC
All India Congress Committee
7, Jantar Mantar Road,
New Delhi-110001

Special Features

(a) Work has been divided into 5 parts:
   (i) Author Index
   (ii) Title Index
   (iii) Classified Index
   (iv) Subject Index
   (v) List of Indian publishers.
(b) Information has been divided in three columns in its each volume.
(c) In Volume-III subject guide the classified subject has been depicted in bold letters.

Physical Format

(a) Its printing is clear which is easily readable.
(b) It is available in three volumes and binding of each volume is hardbound.

Merits

(a) It is the best source of book selection which helps by giving detailed information of books.
(b) It helps in identification of information published in books in India.
(c) It is authentic and reliable source of bibliographical information of Indian books.

(d) Directory of Indian publishers with their complete addresses is given with its each volume.

(e) Key of abbreviation words which have been used in it is also given with each volume.

(f) Subject index is also given along with Vol. III by which information can be easily searched.

(g) Volume I and II have alphabetical arrangement while Volume III has classified alphabetical arrangement which is easy to understand for common readers also.

(h) Bibliographical entries are revised from time to time in it. As a result information given is not always up to date.

Demerits

(a) It provides bibliographical information of English publications in India.

(b) Telephone numbers are not given along with the complete addresses of publishers in 'Directory of Publishers'.

(c) Periodicals, maps, microform, audio-visual material and pamphlets, etc. are not included in it.

(d) Series and ISBN number are not included in information of book entries.

Conclusion: This is very important bibliographical source, which is very useful for Librarians, Documentalists, Information Scientists.

16. Indian National Bibliography

Introduction

It is India's most important bibliography. In this bibliography only current publications are included. The information included in bibliography is reliable and authentic. This bibliography covers current publications in 14 languages including English language. In it only those publications are included which are received by National Library, Kolkata under the Delivery of Books and Newspaper Act of 1954. (Act number 27 of 1954 as amended by Act number 99 of 1956.

Authority

(a) Its publication is done by Central Reference Library under Ministry of Research and Cultural Affairs at the National Library, Kolkata.

(b) Duration of Publication:

(i) The publication of first annual volumes was done in 1958.

(ii) It is published quarterly from 1958 to 1963.

(iii) From 1964 its publication was done monthly.

(iv) From 1967 to 1970 its publication was ceased.

(v) From 1971 to 1977 its publication was irregular.

(vi) From 1984 its publication is continuous and regular.

(c) Its general Editor was B.S. Kesavan.

(d) Indian National Bibliography is divided into two parts:

Part I – General Publication (with Index)

Part II – Government Publication (with index).

Scope

(a) In Indian National Bibliography, current Indian publications covering 14 languages which are obtained under the Act of 1954, are given. The 14 languages are — Bengali, English, Hindi, Sanskrit, Urdu, Punjabi, Kannad, Malyalam, Telulgu, Tamil, Marathi, Gujarati, Assamese.

(b) The following types of publications have been excluded:

(i) Musical scores

(ii) Maps

(iii) Periodicals & newspapers (except the first issue of a new periodicals and the first issue of periodicals under new title).

(iv) Keys and Guides to textbooks

(v) Ephemeral material such as trade catalogue, telephone directory, reports and financial statements of statutory companies, cheap novels, letters and publicity pamphlets.

(c) For outline of the Division of subject of the Dewey and Colon Classification (5th edition) are used in the Indian National Bibliography.

(i) **Divisions of subject by the DDC**

000	General works
010	Bibliography
020	Library Science
030	General Encyclopedia
040	General Collected Essays
050	General Periodicals
060	General Societies, Museums
070	Journalism
080	Collected Works
090	Book Rarities
100	Philosophy
200	Religion
300	Social Science
400	Languages
500	Science
600	Technology and Useful Arts
700	Fine Arts
800	Literature
900	History

(ii) **Main Divisions of the Colon Classification (5th edition)**

z	Generalia
1	Universe of Knowledge
2	Library Science
3	Book Science
4	Journalism
A	Science
B	Mathematical Science
B	Mathematics
I	Physical Science
C	Physics

D	Engineering
E	Chemistry
F	Technology
G	Biology
H	Geology
I	Botany
n	Mining
J	Agriculture
K	Zoology
λ	Animal Husbandry
L	Medicine
M	Useful Arts
μ	Humanities and Social Science
D	Spiritual Experience and Mysticism
V	Humanities
N	Fine Arts
O	Literature
P	Language
Q	Religion
R	Philosophy
S	Psychology
S	Social Science
T	Education
U	Geography
V	History
W	Political Science
X	Economics
Y	Sociology
Z	Law

(d) A list of abbreviations and symbols used is given in INB.

(i) List of symbols (language)

Language Symbols	Language
A	Assamese

Treatment

(a) Full information about a book is given in classified section in following order:

The class number, the author's name, the full title, edition, the place of publication, the publisher, the year of publication, the pages, the kind of illustrations, the size, the nature of binding, the price, the series and annotation wherever necessary. For example:

001 – General Knowledge
Bhatnagar, KB
General Knowledge Encyclopedia, Delhi
Malhotra Bros, 1959, various pagings
22cm, pb. 10.50
(E) z

(b) In it under each main class books are arranged according to sub-subjects. For example:

020 Library Science, General Works
020 Library Science, General Works
020.4 Essays
020.5 Periodicals
020.58 Year Book, director
020.6 Societies, conference, association.

(c) The language of the book is denoted by symbols which are given at the left hand bottom corner of each entry.

(d) The colon numbers are assigned at the right hand bottom corner of each entry against the language symbol.

Srikrishna
Subah Ka Bhula. Delhi, Atmaram and Sons,
1958, 40. illus. 20cm. 1.00
(H) R43

(e) Index – If the author of the book is known, refer to his name in this section and to get the full description of the book go to the classified section by means of the decimal code number given at the end of author entry. For example:

Gopaldas 'Niraj'. *Nadi Kinare*
2nd ed. Delhi. Atmaram & Sons,
1968. 1.50 (H.58) 891.431

Arrangement

(a) Arrangement of INB has been divided into two parts:

I – Classified Part

II – Alphabetical Part

Ist Classified Part

(i) In the classified sequence the entries are arranged by subject according to DDC.

(ii) Colon classification number are also illustrated.

IInd Alphabetical Part

(i) Under each specific subject the name of the author is not repeated and the works are arranged by their titles, *e.g.*

Gandhi, Mahatma Karamchand,
1869 – 1948
Gram seva yam karem, etc.
(H 58)
The Ideology of the Charkha, compiled by
Srikrisna Das Jaju
(E 58)

(ii) Index section contains entries and reference entries under author, title, editor, translator, series and subject in alphabetical sequence.

(iii) List of publishers is also arranged alphabetically.

Special Feature

(a) In INB both DDC and CC schemes are brought into use.

(b) The remain script has been used to represent 14 language symbols.

(c) In it use of bold and italic letters has been done.

(d) In it along with general publication, Government publications are also included.

(e) Bibliography was published in two parts but after Jan. 1973 issue its both parts were amalgamated.

(f) In it below each entry essential notes are given. For example:
Originally published in Bengali as "Swami Sisya Samvad".

Physical Format

(a) Its binding is hardbound
(b) The paper used in it is not of good quality
(c) Its printing is clear and can be read easily.

Merits

(a) This bibliography is most useful for book selection.
(b) INB is useful for research scholars, specialists and library staff.
(c) Through the medium of this bibliography knowledge of publication in many languages can be obtained.
(d) In this bibliography both DDC and CC are used together.
(e) The information given in it is reliable and authentic because in it only those publications are included which are obtained in library under "Delivery of Books and Newspaper Act".
(f) To make the process of search of information easy, index is provided.
(g) In it, only current publications are included.
(h) From 1961 it is being published in different languages to suit different types of readers.
(i) At the last of INB a list with complete address of Indian publishers is given.

Demerits

(a) It is a comprehensive list of all books published in 14 languages. Due to this reason its use gets restricted for person knowing only one language.
(b) At the time of beginning this bibliography it was decided to keep it regular, but this could not happen.
(c) In INB all publications in regional language are recorded

in roman script but most of the Indian readers are unable to understand it.

(d) According to Delivery of Books Act of India, it is necessary that publisher send one copy of their book to Kolkata Library. But sometimes due to certain reasons all publishers are not able to send copy of all their books. So more than 60% Indian publications could not be included in it.

(e) At present along with books, non book material such as disc, floppy, tapes, microforms, etc. are also very informative but such material is not included in INB.

(f) Not all libraries can purchase INB due to its high subscription cost.

(g) Its publication is irregular so information included in it is not uptodate.

Conclusion: INB is most important bibliography which is useful reference source for all kinds of libraries. Along with this it introduces researches, readers, teachers to information of publication in 14 languages.

Other National Bibliographies

1. Asiatic Society. Index to pub. of Asiatic Society.
2. Bhartiya Granth Niketan. Bharat Hindi Granth Suchi, Delhi.
3. Bhartiya Jnanpeeth Pub. Varanasi. Hindi Ke Anumudrit Pub.
4. Bihar Rashtra Shiksha Deptt. Patna. Granth Suchi.
5. Central Institute of Education, Delhi. Bibliography of Periodicals.
6. Gidwari, N.N., Jaipur. Indian Periodicals.
7. Hindustani Academy, Allahabad. Hindi Pustak Suchi.
8. Indian Bibliographical Centre, Varanasi. Indian Books.
9. Indian Bureau of Bibliography, Delhi. Indian Books in Print.
10. Indian Documentation Centre, Gurgaon. Guide to Indian Periodical Literature.

11. Lok Sabha Secretariate, Delhi. List of Govt. Pub. Periodicals.
12. Mukherjee Book House, Kolkata Indian Books.
13. Ministry of Inf. & Broadcasting, Delhi. Press in India. 4 vols.
14. National Information Service, Poona. Guide to Indian Periodicals.
15. Popular Prakashan, Mumbai. Indian Publishers and Booksellers.
16. Rajasthan University, Jaipur. Hindi Sandarbha.
17. Sahitya Academi, New Delhi. National Bibliography of Indian Literature, 1901. 3 vols.
18. Sterling Publishers, New Delhi. Indian Book Industry.
19. Word Press, Kolkata. Indiana.

17. British National Bibliography

London British Library, Bibliographic Service Division
– 1950, Weekly
Edited by A.J. Wells

Introduction

BNB is national bibliography of Great Britain. It is a Government List of all new publications, documents in Great Britain. In it, reliable bibliography of current publications is given. This bibliography is prepared by full cooperation of publishers. Before mass publication, its one copy is sent to British National Museum. Its publication is done to provide knowledge of new publications. Its main purpose is to work in the direction of bibliographical control.

Authority

(a) Its publication is done by Bibliographical Service Division of London.

(b) It is published weekly from 1950.

(c) Following institutions are included in its publication:

  (i) Copyright Department of British Museum

  (ii) Library Association, U.K.

(iii) Association of Publishers and Booksellers.

(iv) ASLIB

(d) Quarterly, monthly, yearly, communicative volumes of this Bibliography are also published.

Scope

(a) Under Copyright Act all published books are included, British Museum, now known as British Library.

(b) Following are excluded:

Periodicals — except those that are new or involve a change of title, musical scores, cheap novelties, maps, certain Government publication, Reprint books.

(c) Only those books are included that are published in English language.

(d) Following things are included:

(i) Essential directions for a proper use of bibliography.

(ii) Outline of the classification scheme

(iii) Table of class number

(iv) Detail of author and title

(v) Subject index

(vi) List of publishers.

Treatment

(a) DDC is used with some modification.

(b) Formation of main entry is according to AACR-II (1967).

(c) Author, title, illustrations, name of publishers, price, size, series, publication, page number are given along with ISBN and BNB numbers.

(d) Title, publisher, price and class number are given in index of BNB.

(e) In it title, index and subject index are given separately.

(f) Chain procedure is used in for constructing subject heading.

Subject Features

(a) Under the Copyright Act of Great Britain, all available published books are included in it.

(b) Earlier, chain procedure was used in it but later on PRECIS was used in it.

(c) Notes are also given in it as required which explains the previous edition.

(d) ISBN and BNB numbers are also given in it.

(e) Bold faced and light faced letters are used in it.

Arrangement

Two types of arrangement are there in BNB:

I – Classified Type

(a) Entries are arranged subject-wise.

(b) Class numbers are given in the notation of DDC.

(c) Now PRECIS is used for providing subject headings.

(d) Main entries are formed according to AACR-II.

II – Alphabetical Part

(a) Author, title, subject, class number, series are included in index.

Its subject index and title index are also arranged alphabetically.

Physical Format

(a) Its binding is of hard board.

(b) Paper used in it is of good quality.

(c) Printing is clear which can be read easily.

Merits

(a) BNB is published regularly.

(b) It is made uptodate from time to time.

(c) BNB is an important and useful instrument for book selection for all libraries because bibliographical information of books is included in it.

(d) This bibliography is helpful in cataloguing and classify the books.

(e) Information given in it is reliable and authentic because books are included in it under Copyright Act.

Demerits

(a) Only English books are included. So it becomes less useful for those who know other languages.

(b) It is very costly; so, many medium size libraries cannot purchase it.

(c) Some publishers get late in submitting their publication in BNB. So, it is not possible to include their publication in.

Conclusion: In view of the above it can be said that BNB is an important reference source for obtaining the knowledge of publications of Great Britain.

Other British Bibliographies

1. Whitaker. London. British Books in Print.
2. Whitaker. London. The Booksellers.
3. Whitaker. London. Cumulative Book list.
4. Times Literary Supplement.
5. British Book News.
6. National Book League. Pamphlet Bibliographies.

American Bibliographies

1. A Checklist of American Imprints.
2. American Book Publishing Record. (Bowker)
3. Books in Print.
4. Evens, Charles. American Bibliography. A Chronological Dictionary of all Books, Pamphlets and Periodicals.
5. National Union Catalogue.

18. Indian Books in Print

Indian Books in Print is an important reference tool. It is published by Indian Bibliographical Bureau, Delhi.

Introduction

It is a list of book or bibliography which gives complete information about the Indian books published every year. It is an annual publication. It includes the following informations:

(a) Name of the book
(b) Title of the book
(c) Translator, if any
(d) Address of the publisher
(e) Price
(f) Size

It is one of the important sources among all reference sources. It is a reliable and authentic source about the information of books published in India every year. It is benefited by the consultation of librarians, research scholars, scientists, businessmen, book traders, publishers, etc.

Authority

Books in Print are published by a famous publisher of the field M/s Indian Bibliographic Bureau, Delhi. Mr. Sher Singh has edited this reference source.

(a) The first edition was published in 1967.
(b) It was published in English in 1980.
(c) This book list is divided in three parts:
  (i) Volume 1 – Author
  (ii) Volume 2 - Title
  (iii) Volume 3 – Subject guide

Scope – It is in three volumes. It includes —

(a) More than 80,000 titles
(b) More than 2,200 Indian publishers
(c) **Volume–I** is author Index. The entry is made according to the single author, joint author, editor, compiler, publisher, place, year, page and price.
(d) **Volume-II** is Title Index. Entries are made according to subject heading in a sequence of title, subtitle, author, edition, place, publisher, year, page and price.
(e) **Volume-III** is a Subject Guide. It includes the informations in the following sequence:

(i) Class Number
(ii) Author / editor / compiler
(iii) Title
(iv) Edition
(v) Place: publisher, year
(vi) Number of pages
(vii) Price

Class number is given according to Dewey Decimal Classification, 16th edition with some modifications.

Example

V.III Subject Guide

<u>General Works</u>	Philosophy
General Knowledge	<u>Religion</u>
Bibliography	Social Science
Library Science	Languages
Essays	Pure Science
General Social	Technology and Useful Art
Museums	Literature
Journals, Newspapers	History, Biography and Travels
Collected Works	
Manuscripts & Rare books	

(f) The list of abbreviations is also given.

Treatment

Volume–I

(a) All honorific words attached with author's name are removed.
(b) The articles 'a, an, the' are also not used with the title.
(c) CCC is used for author, title and edition entry but AACR is used for other informations.
(d) In case of joint author, entry is made in the name of both the authors.
(e) If a book is written by three or more authors, the word

'etc.' will be used after the author's name. Example: AGASME (DS), etc.

(f) If entry is made according to title and author, editor, compiler is not given, the first two letters of the title are given in Block letters.

(g) All added entries are given along with main entry.

Volume–II

(a) Initial articles 'a, an, the' are not used with title entry.

Volume–III

(a) Authors are entered according to CCC.

(b) Subject headings are given according to DDC.

(c) When on specific subject repeats two or more than two authors, the author's name is not repeated.

(d) When there are no readymade subject headings in DDC, the subject headings are constructed or DDC numbers are built.

Arrangement

Volume–I

(a) It is an Author Index which is arranged alphabetically.

(b) All books of one author are also arranged alphabetically.

Volume–II

(a) It is Title Index. All entries are arranged alphabetically. All specific subjects and countries, when referred are arranged alphabetically.

Special Features

In this Directory all works are divided into five points:

(1) Author Index

(2) Title Index

(3) Classified Index

(4) Subject Index

(5) List of Indian Publishers

Every volume is divided into three parts.

In volume three (subject guide) classified subject is written in bold capital letters.

Physical Format

It has a fine printing which can be read easily. It is available in three volumes. Every volume has a hard binding.

Merits

(a) It is an important source of book selection which is helpful in tracing the detail of the books.

(b) It helps in tracing Indian books.

(c) It is an authentic reference source.

(d) There are keynotes of all abbreviations used.

(e) Volume three contains subject index.

(f) Volume one and volume two are arranged alphabetically.

(g) Bibliographical entries are revised from time to time.

Demerits

(a) It is limited to the Indian books only.

(b) It covers only English language books.

(c) It does not mention the complete address and telephone numbers of all publishers.

(d) It does not cover non book material.

However, it is an important reference tool and very helpful to students, faculty, publishers and booksellers and libraries.

(D) ENCYCLOPEDIA

It is a comprehensive work presenting the state of knowledge at a given time concerning the universe or concerning a subject or group of subjects. Most great encyclopedias provide comprehensive under the appropriate heading, and in view of the general availability of these works it is necessary to repeat this information in the present volume. Readers are particularly recommended to study the excellent entries in Brockous and Britannica and to read the very fine general and historical survey of encyclopedia by S.H. Sternbery.

In other words encyclopedia is a book or set of books giving information about all areas of knowledge or about different areas of one particular subject, usually arranged in alphabetical order, a similar collection of information on a CD-ROM.

Encyclopedia as clear from its name, it gives detailed and specific information about world events. It includes all informations regarding man, material, activities, nature, religion, culture and civilization, etc. We cannot define encyclopedia in certain words. It is a creation or a book which gives detailed information about the whole world. A person gets knowledge about the whole world. It includes information of all regions.

Encyclopedia was first prepared and published by Pilri De Elder. It is known as "Enkykliospaideia" in Greek. China published an encyclopedia in 1404-1425 in 119 volumes. German published an encyclopedia in 1818-1889 in 167 volumes.

Greek First published — "Historical Naturals" in 25 volumes.

During 18th century encyclopedias were very much demanded. John Harris published "Lexican Techicum" in England in 1704. Eferan Chambers published 'Chamber's Encyclopedia' in 1705. In 1771 "Encyclopedia Britannica" was started being published and covered the whole area. Its 3 volumes were compiled by William Emilly. The other important encyclopedia "Encyclopedia du XVIII Slecle" was published while in 1796 Germany published "Brockhans Konversations Lexikon" encyclopedia.

Grolier's contribution is well-known in the field of encyclopedia. They published world's second famous encyclopedia "Americana, the Encyclopedia International".

Other important encyclopedias are:

1. Universal Encyclopedia
2. The New Book of Knowledge
3. The American People Encyclopedia
4. The Illustrated Encyclopedia of Child care and Guidance.

During 20th century many encyclopedias were published, out of which Encyclopedia Britannica became the most popular.

(1) Objectives

Encyclopedia has following objectives:

(a) Encyclopedia provides general and specific — all kinds of informations. Its area is whole world.

(b) It is a source of answering the queries. All informations are available in encyclopedia.

(c) Encyclopedia provides all informations relating to persons, materials and activities.

(d) It gives guidance and directions. Every article or detailed account has a list of readings at its end for general reading on the topic.

(e) It removes misunderstanding as informations given in encyclopedias are reliable.

(f) Encyclopedia provides additional informations regarding any subject and general knowledge.

(2) Limitations

Encyclopedias have also limitations of areas and subjects except general encyclopedias.

(a) The information given in encyclopedia is limited to the period of its printing/publishing dates. They become outdated after a period. They are also costly. Their revision is very difficult until and unless there is a permanent team of editors. This has caused to publication of 'supplements' published every year. It is published in limited numbers and sometimes could not be available to the person having the original copy until and unless the collector of original copy could not approach himself for its purchase.

(b) There are many new subjects being generated or grown from time to time which are to be given due place in the encyclopedia which has caused difficulty to retain all old subjects. These encyclopedias provide general informations due to large number of events. They fail to provide full details about the subjects.

(c) Every article/essay has references at its end, but these are mostly outdated and not sufficient as they select few references out of large number of references.

(d) A few encyclopedias have narrow thoughts effected by regionalism, casteism, etc. Some are effected by unqualified staff, lack of expertise of the manpower, editors and network system, etc.

(e) There are a few encyclopedias which are known as world encyclopedias, but they have given more weightage to their own countrymen, religion, culture and events in comparison with other countries, which is essential.

For example: 'Encyclopedia Britannica' and 'The Modern Child Library of Knowledge' have given more details of Christian religion in every volume while very important informations of other religions have been avoided.

An encyclopedia should honour all religions equally.

(3) Kinds of Encyclopedias

There are two types of encyclopedias:

(a) General Encyclopedias

(b) Subject or Special Encyclopedias

(a) General Encyclopedias – In General Encyclopedias, all general informations of all events of the whole universe are given. They do not give importance to a particular subject or their aspects.

(b) Subject or Specific Encyclopedias – They are such encyclopedias which provide informations about a subject or group of subjects.

Example:

(i) Encyclopedia of Physics

(ii) Encyclopedia of Science and Technology.

(4) Qualities of a Good Encyclopedia

While selecting an encyclopedia it is very important that it should cover all informations. While deciding the quality of an encyclopedia, it is necessary to evaluate:

(a) Type of questions to be answered by the informations given in encyclopedia.

(b) Which subject it relates.

(c) Length of articles/essays.

(d) Whether it is fully illustrated to understand an information.

(a) **Editor and Publisher** – A good encyclopedia depends on its editorial ability and editorial board. If the chief editor and other editors are experienced hands and intelligent enough and have a good knowledge of the subject and also popular in the field, then it may be presumed that the encyclopedia will be of a high standard. In addition to this, the writers/authors of the articles/essays should be the persons famous and intelligent in their respective field and their information should be well evidenced.

Publisher has also an important place in the popularity and standard of an encyclopedia. A famous and standard publisher will increase the reputation of the encyclopedia. For example: Many of the editors and writers of Encyclopedia Britannica are national and international awardees.

(b) **Writing Style** – Writing style is an important factor in making an encyclopedia of repute. While compiling an encyclopedia, writing style will have to be more practicable, selection of words, construction of sentences and their clearness, fairness and easiness so that consumer may consult it without the help of the others. Reference librarian may very easily understand the encyclopedia and guide the consumers without any difficulty. If there are a few complex words used, they should be clear and explained by pictures, examples, etc.

(c) **Authentic and Current** – Authentic and current informations make a thing reliable. Such encyclopedias are consulted and referred by all authors and publishers and give benefit to the maximum. Informations are also true which help in researches and readings.

Encyclopedia should be current and up to date. Old and outdated informations make the encyclopedia below standard and do not benefit the consumers. It is a fact that there are events taking place at every moment, hour, day and months in the world. There may be changes in kingdoms at any time. Government changes, natural calamities occur and new inventions are made. All such informations should be made available from time to time and highlighted in encyclopedias.

(d) **Physical get up** – Encyclopedia whether general or subject, its physical features should be well and good, *i.e.* printing, paper, photographs, binding, and size. Printing should be clear, good and quality paper should be used. Attractive pictures, illustrations should be included, and size should be adequate. If all the above qualities are inherent in an encyclopedia, it will be a standard encyclopedia. Durable and attractive binding also add to the beauty of an encyclopedia.

Good physical features attract the users, give them amusement and enable them to concentrate on their studies. It is also beneficial for commercial purpose.

(e) **Index** – Most of the encyclopedias have alphabetical arrangements. Referred names are directed by cross references as it helps in the searching the information. The last volume of encyclopedias is index which helps the reader to trace the information of the events mentioned. It saves the time of the readers.

(5) Evaluation of Encyclopedia

It is necessary to take up the evaluation work seriously and consider all aspects. Encyclopedia is important for commercial and economic purpose. There are factors of evaluation mentioned in "Subscription Books Bulletin". Louis Shore has given following basis of evaluations:

(a) **Importance**

(i) Goodwill of publisher.

(ii) Standard and status of publications.

(iii) Reputation of editors, their experience, education and writings.

(iv) Reputation of co-editors and writers, their experience, education.

(b) **Area**
- (i) Reason of the area (subject)
- (ii) Planning
- (iii) Range
- (iv) Selection of the area
- (v) Comparative basis

(c) **Arrangement**
- (i) Organization
- (ii) Index
- (iii) Study directions

(d) **Use**
- (i) Style
- (ii) For general use or general knowledge
- (iii) Objectivity

(e) **Preparation**
- (i) Binding
- (ii) Paper
- (iii) Type
- (iv) Pages
- (v) Maps
- (vi) Photographs

(f) **Specificity**
- (i) Bibliography
- (ii) Revision
- (iii) Service

(g) **Modernisation** – Encyclopedia should be up to date always. If encyclopedia is not updated with current informations, it will not be used. Supplements are published from time to time or every year mentioning the current informations. Encyclopedias are revised after a certain period.

(6) Important General Encyclopedias

1. *New Encyclopedia Britannica.*

2. *Encyclopedia Americana* (New York: Americana Corp., 1903–). 30 vol.
3. *Collier's Encyclopedia* (New York: Grollier-McMillan, 1949-68). 24 vol.
4. *Encyclopedia International* (New York: Grollier Inc. 1960-65). 20 vol.
5. *Grollier Universal Encyclopedia* (New York: Grolier Inc., 1963–). 10 vol.
6. *American People Encyclopedia* (New York: Grolier Inc., 1948). 20 vol.
7. *Encyclopedia Italiana* (Rome: Ist Dell. Ency., 1949-58). 51 vol.
8. *Australian Encyclopedia* (Michigan Univ., 1948). 10 vol.
9. *Everyman's Encyclopedia* (Dent. 1949-50). 12 vol.
10. *Crompton Encyclopedia.*

(7) Children's Encyclopedias

1. *World Book Encyclopedia.* Chicago: Field Enterprise Edu. Corp., 1917. 2 vols.
2. *Crompton Pictorial Encyclopedia.* Chicago: Ency. Britannica, 1922. 24 vols.
3. *Britannica Junior Encyclopedia.* Chicago: Ency. Britannica, 1934. 12 vols.
4. *New Book of Knowledge.* New York: Grolier Inc., 1910-1966. 20 vol.
5. *American Educator Encyclopedia.* Illinois: United Edu. 1951. 14 vols.
6. *Chamber's Encyclopedia.* Newenes, 1950. 15 vols.
7. *Columbia Encyclopedia.* New York: Columbia Univ., 1951.
8. *Hutchinson's Twentieth Century Encyclopedia.* Hutchinson, 1952.
9. *Newenes Pictorial Encyclopedia.* George Newenes, 1952. 10 vol.

10. *Children Encyclopedia*. Edu. Book Co., 1950-53. 10 vol.
11. *Oxford University Encyclopedia*. Edu. Book Co., 1956-58.
12. *Nelson's Encyclopedia*. Nelson, 1951-63.
13. *Modern Encyclopedia for Children*. Odhams, 1948-54.
14. *Children's New Illustrated Encyclopedia*, 1954.
15. *The Pictorial Encyclopedia*. Samption, 1952.
16. *Modern Children Library of Knowledge*. London: Grollier, 1957-59. 6 vol.
17. *Pear's Encyclopedia*. Odhams Books, 1969.
18. *New Wonder Book Encyclopedia*. Odhams, 1967.
19. *The Book of Knowledge*, 1922. 8 vols.

Other National Encyclopedias

1. *World Mark Encyclopedia of Nations*. New York: Harper, 1960.
2. German: *Konnersatia Laxicon*. Leipzig: Brokham, 1928-35. 21 vol.
3. *Russian: Balshaia Soveskata Cutsiklopdia*. Moskva, 1927-47. 65 vols.; 1949-58. 51 vols.
4. *Canada: Encyclopedia*, Canadian Co., 1965. 10 vol.
5. *French: Grand Larousse Encyclopedia*. New York: French & European Pub., 1960-64. 10 vol.
6. *Spanish: Encyclopedia Universal*. Illustrated Europeo-American (Espasa). Baralona: Espasa, 1905-33. 80 vol.

(8) Indian Encyclopedias

1. *Bangiya Mahakosh*. Calcutta: Indian Research Insti. 1935. 2 nol.
2. *Shishu Bharti*. Calcutta: 1.P.H., 1939-45. 11 vol. (Bengali).
3. *Vishwakosh*. Calcutta: Vishwakosh Press, 1886-1911. 23 vol. (Bengali).

4. *Enyclopedia of India*. Madras: Scotish Press, 1871. 5 vol (English).
5. *Gujarati Gyankosh*. Poona: Ketkar, 1929-31. 2 vol.
6. *Gyan Chakra. One Gujarati Encyclopedia*, Bombay: Capton Ptg. Press, 1918. 9 vol.
7. *Hindi Vishwakosh*. Varanasi: Nagri Pracharni Sabha, 1960-71. 12 vol.
8. *Sachitra Vishwakosh*. Delhi: Rajpal, 1967. 10 vol.
9. *Hindi Vishwakosh*. Calcutta: Vishwakosh Press, 1916-32. 24 vol.
10. *Gyan Gangotri*. Bangalore: Karnatak Coop. Pub. House, 1970. 7 vols. (Kannad).
11. *Kannad Vishwakosh*. Mysore Insti. of Kannad Studies, 1969. 14 vol.
12. *Bal Prapanch*. Bangalore: Satsodhan Prakashan Mandir, 1939. 3 vols. (Kannad).
13. *Viganm*. Trivandrum: Balan Pub., 1956-69. 5 vols. (Malyalam).
14. *Vidyarthi Mitran Malyalam Encyclopedia*. Kottayam: Vidhyarthi Mitram, 1967 (Malyalam).
15. *Vishwa Vijnankosham*. Kottayam: Sahitya Pravartaka Sahrana Sangam. 10 vol. (Malayalam).
16. *Abhinav Marathi Jnankosh*. Kolhapur: K.K. Kulkarni, 1963. 10 vol. (Marathi).
17. *Jnan Parijat*. Bombay: Amar Jyoti Vaugmay, 1964. 2 vol. (Marathi).
18. *Maharashtra Jnankosh*. Poona: Vyavaharik Jnankosh, Mandal. 1920-27. 5 vol. (Marathi).
19. *Sulabh Vishwakosh*. Poona: Vyavaharik Gnankosh, Mandal. 1936-40. 5 vols. (Marathi).
20. *Vishwa Parichay*. Cuttack: Cuttack Pub. House, 1962 (Oriya).
21. *Jnanmandal*. Cuttack: Jnanmandal Prakashan, 1960. 11 vol. (Oriya).

22. *Kalaikkalm Chiyam*. Madras: Tamil Valaicoik Kazakam, 1954-68. 10 vols. (Tamil).
23. *Andhra Vijnanam*. Sarvasvama: Madras, Andhra Patrika Press, 1932. 2 vols. (Telugu).
24. *Andhra Vijnanam*. Kakinad, I.K. Bala Surya. Prasad Rao, 1938-41. 7 vols. (Telugu).

(9) Other Encyclopedias

(a) Encyclopedia on History

1. *World Mark Encyclopedia of Nations*. New York: World Mark Press, 1967. 5 vol.
2. *Dictionary of American History*. N. York: Charls Cribbner, 1940-63. 6 vol.
3. *Encyclopedia of World History*. Baston: Houghton Miffin.
4. *Historical Tables*. Macmillan, 1949.
5. *Annuals of European Civilization*, 1501-1900. Cassell, 1949.
6. *People, Place and Things*. Gibbs-Smith, 1945.
7. *The World We Line In*. Collins, 1957.
8. *The World is Full of Wonders*. Thomas & Hudson, 1967.

(b) Indian Encyclopedias

9. *Vishwa Itihas Kosh*. Bhanpura: Gyan Mandir, 1962-65. 4 vols.
10. *Bhartiya Sanskrit Kosh*. Poona: Bhartiya Sans. Kosh Mandal, 1962. 7 vols.
11. *Bharatvarshiya Prachin Itihasik Kosh*. Poona: Chitrasala Press, 1907-32. 15 vols.

(c) English Literature Encyclopedias

12. *Cambridge History of English Literature*. Cambridge University Press, 1907-32. 15 vols.
13. *A History of Children's Reading and Literature*. Pergamon Press, 1968.

14. *Casellis Encyclopedia of Literature*. Casell, 1953. 2 vols.

(d) Philosophy and Religion

15. *Encyclopedia of Philosophy*. New York: Growell-Collier-Macmillan Pub., 1967. 8 vol.
16. *Encyclopedia of Morals*. London: Bter Oven, 1957.
17. *Concise Encyclopedia of Western Philosophy and Philosophers*. London: Hutchinson, 1960.
18. *Encyclopedia of Religion and Ethics*. Edinburg: Clark, 1908-27. 13 vol.
19. *A History of World Religion*. Bodley Flad, 1966.

Indian

20. *Sivasaram Kathartan Kosh*. Mysore: Granthmala, 1967 (Kannad).
21. *Purana Nighanter*. Kottayam: Gurunathan, 1968. 2 vol.
22. *Purvagthalorhari*. Vijaywada: Ventarma, 1952 (Telugu).
23. *Jainendra Sidhant Kosh*. Delhi: Bhartiya Jnanpith, 1970. 4 vol.

(e) Political Science Encyclopedias

24. *Encyclopedia of Parliament*. London: Cassell.
25. *The Story of Parliament*. London Methuen, 1963.
26. *Indian Parliament*, 1971. Poona: Law Book House, 1971.

(f) Economics and Commerce

27. *Pictorial Encyclopedia of Railways*. Paul Hamlyu, 1968.
28. *Discovery Railway*. University of London Press, 1961.
29. *World Railways*, World Distributors, London, 1963.

30. *The Pocket Encyclopedia of British Steam Locomotives In Colour*. London: Blandford Press, 1968.
31. *The Book of Telecommunications*. London: Murrey, 1962.
32. *Wonderful World*. London: Mcdonald, 1968.

Indian

33. *A Dictionary of Indian Raw materials and Industrial Products*. New Delhi: CSIR, 1948.
34. *Bharat Ki Sampada*. New Delhi: CSIR, 1971 (Hindi).

(g) Encyclopedia on Education

35. *Encyclopedia on Educational Research*. New York: Macmillan, 1960.
36. *Shiksha Vigyan Kosh*. Delhi: Rajkamal, 1967.

(h) Encyclopedia on Art and Architecture

37. *Encyclopedia of the Arts*. New York: Philosophical Library, 1945.
38. *Encyclopedia of World Art*. New York: McGraw Hill, 1959. 15 vols.
39. *Encyclopedia of Hindu Architecture*. London: Oxford, 1927-48. 7 vols.

(i) Encyclopedia on Social Sciences

40. *Encyclopedia on Social Sciences*. New York: Macmillan, 1930. 15 vols.

(j) Science Encyclopedia

41. *Encyclopedia of Science and Technology*. New York: McGraw Hill, 1966.
42. *The Harper Encyclopedia of Sciences*, New York: Harper and Row, 1963.
43. *The International Encyclopedia of Science*. London: Thomas Nelson, 1967.
44. *Nostrand's Scientific Encyclopedia*. New York: Van Nostrand, 1968.

45. *The New Wonder Book of Science*. New York: Ward Lock, 1966.

Other Encyclopedia on Science Subject

46. *Encyclopedia Dictionary of Physics*. New York: Pergamon, 1961-64. 15 vols.
47. *Encyclopedia of Life Science*. New York: Doubleddy, 1961-64. 6 vols.
48. *Encyclopedia of Chemical Technology*. New York: Inter Science, 1911.
49. *Traitede Zoologic*. Paris: Masson, 1948.
50. *Engineering Encyclopedia*, New York: Industrial Press.
51. *Handbuck der Physic*. Paris. 1955.
52. *Newenes Concise Encyclopedia of Nuclear Energy*. London: Newnes, 1962.
53. *Van Nostrand's International Encyclopedia of Chemical Sciences*. London: Princeton, 1964.
54. *Larousee Encyclopedia of Earth*, New York: Promothers, 1961.
55. *Kinzett's Chemical Encyclopedia*. Princeton: Van Nostrand, 1967.
56. *Concise Encyclopedia on Astronautics*. London: Folete, 1968.
57. *Concise Encyclopedia on Astronomy*. London: Folet, 1968.
58. *Manmed Spacecraft; the Pocket Encyclopedia of Space Flight in Colour*. London: Dutton, 1963.
59. *Plant Life in Colour*. London: Odhams, 1964.
60. *Purvell's Encyclopedia of Animal Life*, 1968.
61. *Illustrated Encyclopedia of Animal Life*. London: Odhams, 1967.
62. *Animal Encyclopedia*: Mammals. London: Allen & Urwin, 1948.

63. *Pictorial Encyclopedia of Animal Kingdom.* London: Paul Hamlyn, 1963.
64. *The Living Universe: an Encyclopedia of Biological Sciences.* London: Nelson, 1963.
65. *The Giant Colour Book of Mathematics.* New York: Golden Press, 1960.

Indian Books

66. *Rasayan Darshan.* Vallabh Vidyanagar. Sardar Patel University, 1969 (Gujarati).
67. *Index Therapeutic.* Bombay: Popular Book Depot, 1969.
68. *Television and Radar Encyclopedia.* Bombay: BIP, 1964.
69. *Reactions and Interactions of Drugs.* Bombay: Pestonjor Cooverjee, 1968.
70. *Drug and Therapeutic Encyclopedia of India.* Delhi: Rajpal, 1962.
71. *Pharmacopoeia of India.* Delhi: Manager of Pub., 1966.
72. *Vannaadhi Chandrodaya.* Indore: Gyannandi, 1951-57. 10 vol.

(k) Encyclopedias on Geography

73. *The McGraw Hill Illustrated World Geography.* London: McGraw Hill, 1960–.
74. *The Golden Encyclopedia of Geography.* Oxford.
75. *Geographic Encyclopedia for Children.* London: Paul Hamlyms, 1967.
76. *Geography: Our Planet, its People and Resources.* London: McDonald, 1961.

Indian Books

77. *Geographical Encyclopedia of Ancient and Medieval India.* Varanasi: Indian Academy, 1967.
78. *Aitihasia Sthanavati.* New Delhi: Ministry of Edu., 1969.

Encyclopedias on Music

79. *International Cyclopedia of Music and Musicians*. New York: Dodd.
80. *Grover Dictionary of Music and Musicians*. N.York: Martine Press, 1954. 9 vols.
81. *The Wonderful World of Dance*. London, Rathodone, 1968.
82. *Golden Encyclopedia of Music*. London: Odhams.
83. *Every Child's Book on Music and Musicians*. London: Burke, 1961.
84. *The Wonderful World of Theatre*. London: Rathodone, 1959.

Indian Books

85. *Bangiya – Lokgeet Ratnakar*. Calcutta: PBLSG Parishad, 1967. 4 vols.
86. *Bhartiya Sangeet Kosh*. Calcutta: Kathasilpa, 1965.
87. *Sangit Raga Kalpdrum*. Calcutta, 1916. 3 vols.

(10) Encyclopedia of Library and Information Science

It is an important encyclopedia in the field of library and information science. It was edited by Allen Kent and H. Lancour. M/s Marcel Dekker Inc., New York is a publisher of this encyclopedia and started publishing in 1968.

It covers all subjects, sub-subjects and all aspects of library science. It covers all type of libraries — Public, Academic and Special and their working, library legislation, etc. All informations are arranged alphabetically. Supplements are published every year to make it up to date.

It is an important encyclopedia and informations are reliable. At present it has more than 62 volumes.

(11) International Encyclopedia of Social Sciences

It is an important encyclopedia in the field of social sciences. It is a famous authentic reference work contributed by the social scientists. It is edited by David L. Sills, and published by Macmillan & Co., New York and started publishing in 1968. The edition of 1979 was in 17 volumes and 1992 was in 24 volumes.

It includes:

(a) Anthropology
(b) Economics
(c) Geography
(d) History
(e) Law
(f) Political Science
(g) Psychology
(h) Sociology

It covers the study of historical and analysis material and life sketch also. It covers 69 countries and about 21000 social scientists contributed to this encyclopedia. It provides reliable informations in the discipline of social sciences.

(12) New Encyclopedia Britannica

15th Edition Chicago, Encyclopedia Britannica Inc., Vol. 30, 1985.

Introduction

It is very important and famous encyclopedia of world. It provides information and useful facts. This encyclopedia contains the information of whole universe. This general encyclopedia is reliable source of providing answer of ready reference questions in libraries.

Authority

(a) Its publication is done by Encyclopedia Britannica Inc. Corp., Chicago.
(b) First edition of *Encyclopedia Britannica* come out in 1768 (3 volumes) Edinburgh (Published between 1768-71). At that time its name was "Dictionary of Art and Science" and its publisher was William Smelli.
(c) 14th edition was published under the title "Encyclopedia Britannica" in 1929, USA.
(d) Its 15th edition was published in 1975 in 30 volumes and in 1985 its publication was done in 32 volumes.

(e) The 15th edition was the work of an editorial staff of hundreds and advisory staff more than 200 and more than 4000 contributors.

(f) *Encyclopedia Britannica* consists of 3 parts:

Ist Part – Micropaedia (Ready Reference & Index) in 12 vol.

IInd Part – Macropaedia (Ready Reference & Index) in 12 vol.)

IIIrd Part – Propaedia (outline of knowledge) in 1 vol.

Besides this, 2 volumes — 30 and 31 are in form of Index A-K and L-Z.

Scope

Part I – Micropaedia

(a) In it, about 1 lakh entries are given.

(b) Information is given in brief form in which information related to prominent persons, places, ideas is included.

(c) In Micropaedia following informations are included:

(i) Addenda

(ii) Introduction to statistical summaries

(iii) Comprehensive world statistical tables

(iv) Maps, legend and glossary

(v) Great Charters of the Western World.

(vi) Flags of the countries.

Part II – Macropaedia

(a) About 4,207 articles are there which are descriptive.

(b) Different aspects of knowledge are given in detail.

(c) The articles given are long and descriptive.

(d) Macropaedia contains knowledge in depth providing "more extended treatment of fields of human knowledge and major topics of human interest".

(e) The monographic articles given are on detailed topics covering 22000 pages.

Part III – Propaedia

(a) Propaedia is in single volume, arranged by broad subjects, providing outline of human knowledge, showing relationship between ideas, persons and events.

(b) This volume helps in understanding outline of knowledge and works as guide in getting information from the whole book.

(c) In it, human knowledge has been divided into:

10 Parts
42 Divisions
189 Sections

Part I – Matter and Energy

Introduction of the University of the Physicists, the Chemists and the Astronomers by Nigel Calder

Division I – Atom: Atomic Nucleus and Elementary Particles

111. The Atomic Nucleus; Elementary Particle

Section

112. The Structure and Properties of Atoms

Division II – Energy, Radiation and the States and Transformation of Matter.

121. Chemical Elements: Periodic Variation in their Properties

122. Chemical Compounds

Treatment

(a) In Micropaedia form of Addenda information are given. For example:
Introduction to statistical summaries
Comprehensive world tables
Population data in the ready reference and index
Country statistical tables in the ready reference and index

Comprehensive world statistical tables
World population
Major cities of the world: Population and area
National economics
World transportation
Communications
World education
Major world universities and colleges
Highest mountains of the world
Principle national parks and nature resources
Geographic extremes
Units of measure

Maps

Legend for country: political and physical maps in the Macropaedia
Glossary for the maps
Charters of the Western world
Magna Carta
Bill of Rights
The Declaration of Independence [1776]
Constitution of Rights of Man and of the Citizen

(b) In *Encyclopedia Britannica* headings of articles are divided into sub-headings when and where necessary:

Aatto Alvar	(Heading)
Early work	(Sub-heading)
Nature style	"
Assessment	"
Major works	"

Special Features

(a) Micropaedia

(i) In Micropaedia of *Encyclopedia Britannica* cross references are also given *e.g.* see, see also or q.v. (quod vide for which see....)

World trade: See — Trade International

(ii) In Micropaedia for searching information in other text articles, references are given with articles:

Addison's Prose Style & Fame 1:84a
Advertising Criticism 1:103h
Here, 1 – Volume
84 – Page No.
a – Segment of the page

(iii) In Addenda of Micropaedia footnotes are given:
In World Population and Area
.... No Data available
0 Less than 500
* Latest year available

(iv) In it Glossary and list of abbreviations is also given. For example:
Abbreviation of Language names

Afk	Afrikaans
Alb	Albanian
Ara	Arabic

(v) In *Encyclopedia Britannica* maps, pictures, tables, diagrams, etc. are given according to need.

(b) Macropaedia

(i) In Macropaedia with each article, bibliographies are given.

(ii) To highlight specific information special sub-heading are also given as required.
Example of special sub-headings:
- Important Early Commissions
- Experiments in Furniture

(iii) At the end of each article, brief name of author has been given. For example:
H.F.K.
A.S.K.

(c) Propaedia

In topics of propaedia, according to need, cross references are given which are attached to other parts of sectional outlines or other sectional outline given in propaedia. For example:

Articles	*Article Section*	*Other References*
KINSHIP	7:155b-155hl	5:31f-h/6:1127e-g
10:477-485	7:168g-172d	14:839d-f

(d) In *Encyclopedia Britannica* two kinds of headings and the light face type to portion of related articles covering the subject of entry are given. For example:

Black Faced type
Acton, Lord
Light Faced type
Early training in historical research.

Arrangement

(a) Articles are arranged alphabetically word by word. For example:

Aalto, Alvar
Aaron
Abbas I the Great, of Persia

(b) The number of years are also arranged in words, *e.g.* 1812, Eighteen twelve, war of....

(c) Addenda has alphabetical arrangement of information.

Glossary & Abbreviation

Afk – Afrikaans
Alb – Albanians
Flags of the World
Afghanistan
Albania
Algeria
World Population and area:
 Africa
 Algeria, Angola, Benin
 America South
 Argentina, Bolivia, Brazil
Major World Universities and Colleges:
 Africa
 Algeria
 Algiers, University of
 Constantine, University of
 Asia

India
Agra University
Aligarh Muslim University
Allahabad, University of
Calcutta, University of
Delhi, University of

Highest Mountain of the World:
Africa
Kilimanjaro, Tanzania
Kenya, Kenya

Longest rivers of the World:
Nile
Amazon
Africa
Nile
Congo
Niger
America, North
America, South
Asia
Europe

Physical Format

(a) Binding is of hard board.

(b) Printing is clear and bold letters are used in it.

(c) Paper is of good quality.

(d) It can be easily consulted while keeping on table.

Merits

(a) To keep this encyclopedia uptodate "Britannica Book of the Year" and "World Data Annual" are published every year.

(b) Along with general knowledge, geographical information biography of prominent personalities is also given.

(c) Through this encyclopedia all type of queries can be answered.

(d) From the reference point of view presence of New Encyclopedia is essential. This helps in giving ready reference service and knowledge on historical topics to users.

(e) At the end of each article bibliography has been given. If user wants to get information in detail, he can get aid from this bibliography.

(f) To make information reliable and authentic, at the end of each article name of author is given in initial form. And the whole information about the author can be obtained from index volume.

(g) Language is easy and thus a common user can easily search in it.

Demerit

(a) In each branch of knowledge new development and experiments are occurring everyday, in such a situation it becomes difficult to arrange all the information systematically.

(b) To publish new edition of Britannica lot of money and labour is required. This is the reason due to which its editions are not published frequently and information becomes absolute after some time.

(c) No doubt to make the encyclopedia up to date per year, year book is published but then also it is unable to provide complete or whole information.

(d) In propaedia, arrangement of entries is difficult to understand by a common user.

(e) Britannica is costly; due to this reason, all libraries cannot purchase it.

Conclusion: This encyclopedia is very useful reference tool for all type of users and libraries. Information related to every field of knowledge in the world is given.

(13) Encyclopedia Americana

New York, Grolier, Vol. 30, 1987.

Introduction

The main object of this encyclopedia is to provide information of the whole world. This is very important and useful encyclopedia. This is a tool to get up to date and standard information of various branches of knowledge from all over the world.

Authority

(a) It is published by Grolier Pub., New York.

(b) Its first edition was published between 1829-1833 and it was based on the German encyclopedia named "Borckhaus Konversation – Lexikon" (1827-29).

(c) In 1920 it was published in 30 volumes.

(d) For preparing this encyclopedia about 6000 authors contributed.

(e) This encyclopedia is divided into 3 parts.

Scope

(a) About 70,000 articles are included.

(b) General information of science and technology, new branches of science, social science, humanities, religion etc. is given.

(c) It also includes biographies of persons.

(d) It contains about 3,50,000 entries.

(e) It contains key to abbreviations and Index.

(f) It also includes about 18,000 illustrations.

Treatment

(a) In it, headings are given in bold faced type and use of symbols is done at places.

(b) In this encyclopedia both types of articles — brief and detailed are included.

(c) The name of author is given in abbreviated form at the end of the article and at the start of the first part, full list of the name of authors is provided.

Special Features

(a) This encyclopedia includes the vocabulary of technical words.

(b) Footnotes are provided at the end of entries.

(c) For specifying the subjects, important data maps and diagrams are given.

(d) For making it uptodate "The Americana Yearbook" is published.

(e) For special study a selective bibliography is provided at the end of each article.

(f) In it, special articles are collected for explaining difficult words and the subject related to it.

Arrangement

(a) The arrangement of information is alphabetical.

(b) Its index is arranged alphabetically.

(c) The key to abbreviations is also arranged alphabetically.

Physical Format

(a) It is hardbound.

(b) Fine quality paper is used.

(c) Its printing is clear and the illustrations are provided as needed.

Merits

(a) It includes general information as well as information to subject.

(b) It has used simple language for providing knowledge to common man.

(c) This encyclopedia is useful for all types of readers because it includes almost all the subjects.

(d) For making information authentic, the abbreviated name of the author is given at the end of each article.

Demerits

(a) This reference tool is very costly therefore all the libraries cannot subscribe it.

(b) The information provided in it is mainly concerned with America.

(c) For making this encyclopedia up to date publication of yearbook is done but even then also many informations are left from being included in it.

Conclusion: This encyclopedia is useful and important tool for all types of libraries and provides information related to all subjects.

(14) Encyclopedia of Library & Information Science (New York: Dekker, 1968) Vols. 1-35

Introduction

It is a special type of encyclopedia in which all information relating to Library Science are included. Its main objective is to compile all important informations related to Modern events and trends in library and information science. It is an important source in the field of library and information science.

Authority

Encyclopedia of Library and Information Science was published by Marcel Dekker, New York. The first thought of its publication came in mind in 1966. It started being published in the end of 1966 under the editorship of Allen Kent and Harald Lancour. It is now published in 54 volumes. It has supplementary volumes after two years.

Scope

Encyclopedia of Library and Information Science includes the detailed study of all type of libraries (Public, academic, special) of the world. There are essays on all aspects of libraries. It also includes:

(a) Famous librarians.

(b) Famous Lib. & Inf. Sc. teachers.

(c) Famous important personalities of the field of Lib. & Inf. Science.

(d) It has given an account of life of important personalities, who have given their valuable contribution in the field of libraries.

Index – The last volumes are Index. The whole Encyclopedia covers 35 thousand pages.

Treatment – There is a mention of life sketch of the authors and also references which may make the readers aware of the related literature.

The Index is divided into two parts:

(a) Author Index

(b) Subject Index

Indexes include cross reference also. This encyclopedia also gives details of computer printing.

It also gives detailed study of the pioneers of library science like Ranganathan, Dewey, Cutter and others.

Special Features

The encyclopedia of Library and Information Science has the following special features:

(a) Data, Graphs, Diagrams, Index, tables are also used in the text.

(b) It has supplementary volumes published to include and provide latest informations. Its frequency is 2 years.

(c) It has a summary of all essays.

(d) It includes references wherever necessary.

Arrangement

The arrangement in encyclopedia of library and information science is alphabetical under the subject headings.

The index is also alphabetically arranged.

Physical Format

(a) It has a Rexin binding.

(b) It is an authentic and reliable encyclopedia in the field of Library and Information Science.

(c) This encyclopedia is useful to the librarians, scientists, bibliographers, documentalists, analysists, researchers, students and teachers.

(d) It is the first encyclopedia of Library and Information

Science which is complete and informative as it gives detailed study and history of all events in details.

Demerits

Though all efforts are being made to uptodate it by publishing supplement volume, even then there are many informations left and not included.

However, it is an important encyclopedia and useful to all libraries.

(15) McGraw Hill Encyclopedia of Science and Technology

It is published by McGraw Hill Publishing Co., New York.

Introduction

It is multivolume encyclopedia. It covers the field of Natural Science, Technology, and Applied Sciences.

Its informations are Authentic and reliеble. Its gives detailed account of all events and working in the field of Science and Technology.

Authority

(a) It is a publication of McGraw Hill Publications. Its first edition was published in 1960.

(b) It has been published in 8 editions.

(c) More than 3000 scientists have contributed to this encyclopedia, out of them some are Novel prize winners.

Scope

(a) It covers Biology, Physics, Zoology, Engineering, etc.

(b) It does not include historical, philosophical and biographical information until and unless referred in the text matter.

(c) It does not include medical sciences.

(d) It includes psychological essays.

(e) It has two indexes:

   (i) Analytical – it includes 2 lakhs entries in its latest edition.

(ii) Topical Index – it includes 77 main subjects with 7500 essays with titles.

Treatment

(a) There is a list of books referred after every essay.

(b) There are tables, charts, diagrams, data and statistics used to describe the problems and matter.

(c) There are full page maps given.

(d) In addition to above, formulas, chemical analysis, reaction scheme, mathematical equations are also given when necessary.

(e) Sub-headings are given in bold letters.

(f) There is a mention of the writer after every essay along with his know-how and experience.

Arrangement

(a) In this encyclopedia, matter is arranged alphabetically.

(b) Analytic Index entries are arranged word by word.

(c) Topical entries are arranged alphabetically.

Physical Format

(a) It has a rexin binding.

(b) Printing is clear.

(c) Paper is of high quality.

Merit

(a) It gives all information related to science and technology.

(b) It helps in answering the reference queries related to science and technology.

(c) There is a regular publication of McGraw Hill yearbook and science and technology yearbook to make the encyclopedia up to date.

(d) There are more than 800 scientists contributing to the supplement yearbooks.

(e) It is helpful to scientists, technologists and also libraries.

Demerits

(a) Though it is uptodated by publishing yearbooks, even then many informations still need to be included.

(b) It is limited to science and technology field.

Conclusion – It is an important source of information of science and technology field. It is beneficial to the libraries, teachers and students.

(E) BIOGRAPHY

Biography means the story of a person's life written by others. It is a natural desire of man to narrate his life events to others and also study the events of others life and his experiences. In this way it records the informations about the experiences and events. Many wise men/academicians say:

It is necessary to know before studying life history as to what is biography (like sketch). Thomas Karlail has defined bibliography as the life sketch of a person. In Greek, the word "Bios" or "Grapo" means 'life' and 'writing' respectively. In other words writing about the life of a man. Biography is a statement of life that has been actually lived. Huiden says – 'To write about the life of a person is called biography.'

As per Chambers Encyclopedia – It is a branch of knowledge in which the history of a special person is mentioned.

According to *Encyclopedia Britannica* – Biography is a statement which mentions or writes the record of activities, personality and contribution of a person. It mentions detailed informations of the life events like historical events.

Therefore, Biography or Biographical dictionary mentions the events of a group of persons or the individual person having special contribution to the society.

Biographies may be divided into two kinds:

1. Autorbiography – The biography which is written by a person about his own life.
2. Biography – The biography is written on a person by some other persons.

The first biography was written in 17th century by Dryden known as "Plutorch's Life". Similarly Issac Walter wrote "Life Doue" in 1940 and Boswell's "Life of Johnson" in 1961. But biographies were really demanded in 20th century when many biographies were published. In 1968 Stratch wrote "Eminent Victorious".

There are many readers who demand informations about the life, activities, religious works, philosophical views, writings, entertainment, relations, family life, education and death of a person. There are many informations specially highlighted in a biography like date of birth, educational life, family members and the address. Biography mentions all such informations.

(1) Kinds of Biography

Biography is of many kinds:

(a) Biography of famous persons

(b) Biography of subject specialists

Other Categories

(a) General and universe biographies

(b) National and regional biographies

(c) Commercial and subject biographies

(d) Modern biography

All above biographies provide informations of their specific fields. Biographies are published in many volumes even then it could not cover all important persons. The question is what is the limit of the persons included. There are biographies which mention limited persons of a specific field, subject, country or region. All bibliographies help the Reference librarian to provide informations about the important persons to the readers. Biographies of subject specialists provide detailed account of scientists, social scientists, economists, politicians and religious leaders. Regional biographies are very important. There are many informations demanded or required by the readers about the persons of the region. For example: Persons of America, Persons of India, etc. All such informations are available in Regional biographies which provide detailed account of the persons of the region. Geographical and commercial biographies provide informations of the persons relating to author — apologists, geographers, traders, industrialists, businessmen, technical persons, etc.

Biographics are revised every year. There are biographies which include only living persons while a few biographies include living and also dead persons.

(2) Evaluation of Biographies

There are many biographies. It is not possible to acquire all biographies. Therefore, only few important biographies are selected bibliography. Such biographies are selected on the following grounds:

(a) **Authority** – There are many important persons which are not mentioned in reference books. If mentioned that is not detailed informations. Such informations are mentioned in a few biographies, *i.e.* name of the writer, editor and subject of the life. In fact biographies are media of detailed informations of a persons, his activities, place, etc. For example — Dr. Homi Jahangir Bhabha an atomic research scientist is famous for atomic science. Biography of science field or general bibliography has mentioned a detailed account of the life and contribution of Dr. Bhabha which is useful to the readers for their knowledge. Hence, the name of the editor, the publishers are two factors to evaluate a biography.

(b) **Arrangement** – While evaluating a biography whether standard one, it is necessary to judge the bibliographical details, their arrangements, *i.e.*

(i) Chronological order

(ii) Alphabetical order

(iii) Subject order

(c) **Selection of notable persons** – A biography mentions detailed account of life of important persons. There are bibliographies in which national persons are mentioned and foreigners are avoided. On the other hand there are important persons included in one bibliography while avoided in other bibliography. Therefore, the persons and their detailed information determines the importance and standard of a bibliography.

(e) **Problems** – There are a few problems while preparing a biography, such as:

(i) **Name of the persons** – There are many persons with similar names which create confusion. They differ by date of birth, place of birth, educational institutions etc. The other solution is to mention them by surname entry. For example. There are many persons with name Rajendra Prasad who can be a writer, musician or the President of a nation. Thus, the specificity of a man can be presented by their work.

(ii) **Unknown person** – There are few questions which cannot be answered by the readers until and unless the information about the full name of the person, his date of birth, birth place is not known. Subject bibliographies mention all such informations and satisfy the readers. Sometimes the reader needs information about subject experts which can be available in subject bibliography.

(3) Dictionary of National Biography

It is edited by S.P. Sen and published by Institute of Historical studies. It was first published in 1972 in 4 volumes.

It is an important national biography. It covers details of economic, social, cultural, political, educational, scientific and technological persons living or dead. Informations are written by the academicians. It includes more than 20000 entries. Persons are arranged alphabetically. But the persons which are famous with their personal name are mentioned as usual.

It is an important reference tool.

(4) India's Who's Who

It is an INFA publication, New Delhi and was published in 1969. It is Annual publication.

Introduction

Its first edition was published in 1969 and being published regularly. It is running its 28 editions.

Scope

(a) In this reference source the life-sketch of such persons have been studied who have contributed something special for nation and achieved a special place in the society by their services and works.

(b) It has included 5000 famous personalities of 120 fields of services.

(c) Every year more than 400 entries are added.

(d) All informations given in this reference source are useful to the government, workers, teachers, scientists, travellers, etc. Some new fields are also included in it.

(e) It includes organizers, vice-chancellors, justice, etc.

(f) It contains a list of abbreviations.

(g) It is divided in 7 parts. All parts contain details of the persons of all fields.

(h) Seven parts are:

  (i) Related to common society, *i.e.* Central Govt., State Govt., Foreign policies.

  (ii) Trade, *i.e.* private and public trade, industrial management, finance, labour, etc.

  (iii) Humanity – Arts, disabled persons, design, education, literature, etc.

  (iv) Science – Zoology, Chemistry, Physical Science, Maths, etc.

  (v) Applied Science – Agriculture, Technical, Engineering, Medical Science, etc.

  (vi) Social Science – Social, Economical, Philosophy, Human, etc.

  (vii) General – Archaeology, Hotel, Travel, Library and Information Science, Museum, Printing, Yoga, Sports, etc.

Treatment – All details given in this reference source are exhaustive and brief. The details are as under:

(a) Full name

(b) Date of birth

(c) Postal address

(d) Education

(e) Profession/occupation

It has two kinds of index:

1. Index of the persons which is arranged according to the surname of the person.
2. Index of advertisers.

Special Features

It is published every year. Latest informations are added ever year. Special informations or such informations which are to be highlighted are put in the bold letters.

Arrangement

Index is arranged according to the surname of the persons and that is alphabetical.

All details/text are arranged under the subject.

Special Format

It has clear printing. Paper used is of high quality. It has a hardboard binding.

Merits

(a) It is a biographical source.

(b) It is kept uptodate.

Demerits

(a) It covers the biography of Indians only.

(b) It is published every year so as to keep it uptodate. Even then it does not cover all important persons.

(5) International Who's Who

It is international biographical reference sources. It is published by Europa Publications. It is published annually since 1935.

Introduction

Biographic word is a word of Greek language which means Bio = relating to life and Graphic = writing. In other words Biography means life-sketch of a person. Louis Shores has put the International Biographies an important reference source. It is directory of important persons which is arranged alphabetically according to surname.

Authority

It is published by Europa Publications Ltd., London. Its first edition was published in 1935 and is being published continuously since then.

Scope

This biography includes the following famous persons of the world:

(a) Scientists
(b) Teachers
(c) Administrative Officers
(d) Political Leaders
(e) Sportsmen

It covers important persons of 120 countries, whose life has been described and their list is given in brief.

Treatment

In this reference tool the following informations are given about the persons mentioned in this source:

(a) Full name — surname, forename
(b) Designation
(c) Nationality
(d) Education
(e) Present position
(f) Permanent address
(g) Telephone number
(h) Honours/awards

Special Features

(a) Persons mentioned in this reference source, if not alive, the information is given in a special column.
(b) It includes information about royal families also.

Arrangement

(a) Information is arranged alphabetically according to the surname of the person.

(b) The list of abbreviations used is also arranged alphabetically.

Physical Format

(a) It has a hardboard binding.

(b) It has a clear print.

(c) The paper used for its print is of good quality.

Merit

(a) It is published every year to make it up to date.

(b) It also gives information about subjects and fields.

(c) The persons who are using pseudonym name, their actual name is also given.

Demerits

(a) It includes majority of persons of European countries in comparison with Asian persons.

(b) It is a biographic source in English language.

(c) It is less important to the readers of other languages other than English.

Conclusion – International Who's Who is an important source of information. It is useful to libraries and library reference services.

(6) Important Biographies

1. *Webster's Biographical Dictionaries*. London: Marian Co., 1903.
2. *Universal Pronouncing Dictionary of Biography and Mythology*. London: Lippincott, 1930.
3. *New Century Cyclopedia of Names*. New York: Appleton Century Croft, 1954.
4. *Biographic Universale*. Paris: B. Desplaces, 1943.
5. *Who's Who*. New York: Wilson, 1951.
6. *Current Biography*. New York: Wilson, 1940.
7. *International Who's Who*. London: Europa, 1935.
8. *International Yearbooks and Statesmen Who's Who*. London: Burkles Peerage, 1953.

9. *Dictionary of National Biography*. Calcutta: Institute of Historical Studies. 1972.

(F) MAPS AND ATLAS

Atlas is the collection of maps and informations. Maps mention the informations of area, rivers, mountains, lakes, oceans, ways, deserts, roads, rails, etc. Globes are also helpful to provide such informations. ALA Glossary defined — Atlas is a collection of maps and engraved style and index of the informations.

Maps fulfil the object of tourists, etc. It is included in reference books. Maps are used at the level of schools and it helps in providing knowledge to the readers in a library. Libraries maintain Maps at a special place and in a different manners. Maps answer the queries of the readers relating to natural places and geographical physical and natural places, etc. They present and highlight the events of the whole world. National boundaries are also mentioned in maps. All maps are published after the approval and consent of the Government. Thus informations given in maps are reliable.

(1) History

Cartography is an art. It is not a work of an ordinary artist to cartograph the maps, colour combination, exact position of the places, etc. Only expert and experienced hand cartographers draw the maps. The first cartographer was from Alexandria in 150 AD who prepared a map "Geographia" in 8 parts. Merketer is known as Godfather of cartography. He collected 107 maps in 1595. He developed maps in Medieval period. During 17th century cartography developed in Spain, France, England and America. Maps are not always prepared for some purpose but for other works also. Maps are the media of expression. They highlight problems, events, geographical situations also.

(2) Kind of Maps

(a) According to Form:

(i) Physical maps

(ii) Political maps

(iii) Historical maps

(b) According to size:

(i) Enlarged maps

(ii) Abridged maps

(iii) School maps

(c) According to colours:

(i) Plane maps

(ii) Coloured maps

(iii) Lining maps

(d) According to regions:

(i) World maps

(ii) National maps

(iii) Regional maps.

(3) Evaluation of Maps

Evaluation of maps is based on following points:

(a) Graphical Art

(b) Mathematical Presentations

(c) Compilation and editing

(d) Uptodateness

(a) **Graphical Art** – A cartography is an art which is technical and training helps in preparation of Atlas. There are special organizations and institutions preparing Atlas. They engage experienced hand and trained cartographers for this work. A few organizations are famous for preparation of atlas and their atlases are considered most reliable and authentic.

(b) **Mathematical Presentation** – The reliability depends on the mathematical presentation of the atlas. Mathematical statistical analyses, measurements, clarity, facts and figures are the basic authenticity of an atlas. There is a need of accuracy of distance between places, mountains, length of rivers, details of media of transportations and border of the countries, states, districts, etc. Therefore, there should be no mistake in calculations, measurements and their presentations as it may create problem and dispute between two countries, states, etc. Therefore, it needs experts to prepare atlas and get certified by the Government.

(c) **Compilation and editing** – Compilation of Atlas is a work of special character. Good compilation increases the importance of Atlas. An Atlas can be of high standard if it is compiled by experienced hand and trained cartographers. Editing is also an important factor for a good Atlas. A decorated, illustrated, durable colours, graphs, index and charts enhance the quality of a Atlas. A good atlas help the reader in his study and research.

(d) **Location** – Geographical positions are changed. Changes occur time to time in political situations, agreements, election areas, boundaries of state, district, cities, roads and historical places. We survey such events that happen every year or five years or a decade. Atlas includes all such changes in its maps from time to time. For example. India after partition, Russia in the reign of Stalin, independences of Tanzania and Janjibar, and Bangladesh, there have been changes in the names of places, lakes, rivers and historical places. Many boundaries have been changed. Maps are also changed according to changes.

Maps also highlight the developments of countries. Maps present new roads, rail lines, rivers, dams, increase in production, decrease in production, rainfalls, mines, minerals, etc. Therefore, maps should be revised accordingly.

(e) **Decorative**

(i) **Scale** – Maps should have clarity, and fact-findings scale is the basis of a map. Scale may be small or large, it determines the size of the map. It makes the map more understandable. A real presentation of scale makes a map standard.

(ii) **Colour** – Maps are prepared in many colours like green, red, yellow, blue, black and also with different lines in different colours. Dark colour lines for railways and roads, dark spots for cities and small stations.

(iii) **Symbols** – Signs and symbols are used to represent rivers, lakes, villages, cities, roads, rails, parks, airports, historical places so that reader may trace the location.

(iv) **Type** – Attractive type letters are used for printing of maps. Different typed letters are used for places, rivers, mountains, provinces, ocean, sea, etc. Simple, plane, bold, italic type letters are used.

(f) **Uptodate** – All Atlases and maps should be uptodated time to time so that readers may be aware of the latest informations.

(g) **Binding** – There should be durable binding. Leather binding will be more useful as maps and Atlases are utilized for many years. Good and durable binding makes an Atlas more safe and protected. Good and shining colours of a Atlas help the readers to identify the Atlas of his choice.

(4) Important Maps and Atlases

1. *Times Atlas of the World*. London: Times. 5 vols. (19½:12:240).
2. *National Geographic Atlas of the World*. Washington: National Geographic Society. (19:12½:113).
3. *Index in Maps*. N.Delhi: Publication Division 1951.
4. *Survey of India Atlas*. Dehradun: Survey of India, 1954.
5. *National Atlas of India*. Calcutta: National Atlas org.
6. *Subject Atlas*. New York: Berues & Noble, 1964.
7. *Atlas of World History*. Chicago: Rand McNally, 1957.
8. *Atlas of American History*. New York: Charles: Scriber.
9. *Historical Atlas of Indian Peninsula*. Bombay: Oxford University Press, 1959.
10. *Indian Agricultural Atlas*. Delhi: Manager of Pub., 1950.
11. *Indian Cotton Atlas*. Delhi: ICAR, 1959.

(5) The Great World Atlas

Introduction

It is one of the most important geographical reference sources of world from which information of all geographical areas of world can be obtained. Information given in it are authentic and reliable. This reference source is very useful through the medium of which we can get geographical information for locating place, city, state, mountain river, forest, etc.

Authority

(a) Its publication is done by DK (Dorling Kindersley) Ltd., London.

(b) Its first edition come out in 1999 and second edition was published in 2002.

(c) In its creation many editorial staff and consultants contributed which are as follows:

Editorial Staff — 12

General Geographical Consultants — 3

Regional Consultants — 10.

Scope

(a) The way of using this Atlas is given under "How to use this Atlas".

(b) In it, all geographical information of universe is given for *e.g.* solar system, the physical world, structure of earth, shaping the landscape, the world's oceans, the global climate, life on earth, population and settlements, the economic system, the political world, states and boundaries, international disputes, etc.

(c) Under "Index Gazetteer", countries of the world, geographical philosophy, geographical comparison geographical names and index are given.

(d) Satellite image maps of all countries of world are given, under which following countries are included North America, Africa, Europe, Asia, Australia, Oceania.

(e) Greenwich time of world is included under "Time zone Maps".

(f) In it, under "countries of world" 193 independent countries and 51 dependencies are included.

(g) Divided countries of Soviet Union 1991 and 1992 Yugoslavia are also included in it.

Treatment

(a) In this Atlas maps are arranged in following way: The world, the political continents, continental resources, the physical continents, regional mappings, satellite image mapping, etc.

(b) Following information are included under geographical information: Forest, mountains, desert, animals, ancient plants, international trade flow, world money market, tourism.

(c) Geographical comparison of countries of world is given under which following informations are included: Largest countries, smallest countries, largest islands, richest countries, poorest countries, most populous countries, least populous countries, most widely spoken language, countries with most land borders, longest rivers, highest mountains (height above sea level), Greatest waterfalls (mean flow of water), highest waterfalls, largest desert, hottest inhabited places, driest inhabited places, wettest inhabited places, etc.

(d) Special features shown on regional and continental maps and list of names of places is given in index *e.g.*

272J7 Himachal Pradesh <> State NW
NW India
Himalaya/Himalaya Shan see Himalayas

Under "countries of world" special and general information related to each country is given such as official names, formation capital, population, total area, languages, region, government, currency, literacy rate.

INDIA

South Asia

Official name	–	Republic of India
Formation	–	1947
Capital	–	New Delhi
Population	–	1 billion, 1883 people per sq. mile (341 people/sq.km)
Total Area	–	1,259,338 sq. miles (3,287,590 sq.km)
Language	–	Hindi, English, Bengali, Marathi, Telugu, Tamil, Kannada and others.
Religions	–	Hindu 83%, Muslim 11%, Christian 2%, Sikh 2%, Buddhist 1%, Other 1%.
Ethnic mix	–	Indo Aryan 72%, Dravidian 25%, Mongoloid & others 3%.
Government	–	Parliamentary, Democracy
Literacy rate	–	57%
Calorie Consumption	–	2417 Kilo cal./person
Currency	–	Rs. = 100 paisa

Special Features

(a) With each map, general key, map key, glossary, scale, the transportation and industry, urban and rural population are given which represent different types of special features of continent such as communication, physical features, drainage features, settlements, borders, miscellaneous features.

(b) Glossary of abbreviations is given. The glossary presents a detailed study of abbreviations used in Atlas and index.

(c) At the end of this Atlas flags of all countries of world are given with country's name and page number.

(d) According to need, footnotes are also given.

(e) Satellite image maps of world are given.

(f) Maps provide unique view of today's world which are attached by new digital technology along with traditional cartographic technique.

(g) Colours are used to display various natural elements.

Arrangement

(a) **Continental Arrangement** – In this Atlas, maps are arranged continent by continent.

(b) **Alphabetical Arrangement:**

(i) Geographical glossary and index are alphabetically arranged.

(ii) Countries of the world are arranged alphabetically.

Physical Format

(a) Binding is of hardboard.

(b) Paper used is of good quality.

(c) Printing is clear and maps given in it are coloured.

Merits

(a) Great World Atlas is an important geographical reference source through the medium of which important information can be known and we can also know about smallest unit of the world.

(b) It is useful for all types of readers specially related to geography.

(c) It is very authentic and reliable source for ready reference service.

(d) To include latest information its revised editions are published from time to time.

Demerits

(a) Name of geographical places and their political boundaries are subject to constant change. To bring changes immediately in Atlas is impossible. The size of this Atlas is quiet large which creates problem in its easy consultation.

Conclusion – It is an important reference source for each and every reader and the library. It is a medium to get easily geographical information.

(G) DICTIONARY

Dictionary contains the words of a language or subject arranged in an alphabetical arrangement giving their meaning, spelling, pronunciation and derivation. The word Lexicon, thesaurus, word book, vocabulary and glossary are also used as synonyms for dictionary. It is of many types:

(a) Language dictionary
(b) Subject dictionary
(c) Special purpose dictionary like:
  (i) Spelling dictionary
  (ii) Synonyms dictionary
  (iii) Dictionary of new words.

However, it is a book that gives a list of the words of a language in alphabetical order and explains what they mean, or gives a word for them in a foreign language. It is also a book that explain the words that are used in a particular subject. It includes a list of words in electric form.

Dictionary means words + kosh, *i.e.* collection of words. Thus, collection of words of a language is called dictionary. Dictionary includes:

(a) Meaning of words
(b) Pronunciation
(c) Grammar rules
(d) Synonyms
(e) Definitions
(f) Abbreviations
(g) Similar words in other languages
(h) Usage
(i) Slang
(j) Dialect
(k) Spelling

Dictionary has a wider area. It includes the words of all subjects, languages, nature, persons, or place names, etc.

Dictionary is an important reference book. Readers require word meaning at every point of language problems or while expressing his views, which is provided by dictionaries.

(1) History

Language originated with the origin of man. Language has been a media of message conversion among the men whether it is in signs, symbols or other media as clear from Sumer tablets. For the first time a list of clay tablets was prepared which was in defective language and used by limited community. Churia prepared a dictionary in ancient period which was 1000 years early to BC which was having more than 35000 signs and symbols. There are no indications of writing such dictionary in Roman and Greek. Academicians also have different views. In India Sanskrit dictionaries were prepared in which the famous dictionaries are Amar Singh's "Amar Kosh" and 'Namaloga Nusasan'. They were prepared due to effort and encouragement of Raja Vikramaditya.

Dictionary was named after the Latin word "Dictionariam" which was first spoken in English by John De Goledika. There were two dictionaries written in 14th and 15th century:

(a) Peter Barkorius's "Dictionariam Morale Utrsgue Testamenti".

(b) "Anglo-Saxon of Latin words".

These dictionaries have meanings of Latin words in English language.

Popularly dictionaries were written and used in 17th century when small dictionaries were produced. The first English dictionary was written in 1604 by Robert Kohra entitled "A Table Alphabete". The other dictionary was "Universal Etymological Dictionary" by Netherian Belley in 1721 in which all words of daily usage were given. In the same period Edward Phillips wrote a dictionary "New World of English Words". This dictionary attracted the readers and this effort resulted into writing another dictionary prepared by

Samual Johnson. He gave the details of the words in addition to their meanings which can provide more informations to readers. He took 8 years to write another dictionary and completed it in 1755 with the title "A Dictionary of the English Language", which included many new words being used in 18th century. It is known as an important dictionary and sold in thousands copies. It had grammatical explanations and usage style.

The contribution of Nohe Bekster is also important in the field of dictionaries. This dictionary was an example of developed style of usage of words. Its details attracted the readers. It was widely used. This dictionary was entitled "A Compendious Dictionary of the English Language" in 1806. This was the first dictionary which gave both American and English words separately and words were analysed properly and accurately. Its first edition was limited to schools only. In 1828 Bekster wrote a large dictionary entitled "An American Dictionary of English Language". It was a unique dictionary and it had no comparison. It was published by the famous publisher G.C. Merium & Co., which made extraordinary efforts to enlarge it. He took publication rights and published a large dictionary "Webster's Third New International Dictionary" in 1909. Its 4th edition was published in 1934, 1961, and 1971 with meaning of words in 6 languages. It is the best dictionary of the world and published in 3 volumes.

Since 1957 about 5000 academicians made a collection of English words for a period of 20 years in England. There were more than 50 lakh words and a dictionary was prepared and published entitled "Fosters Dictionary" 2 vols. and Carry's Dictionary 2 vols.

During 20th century dictionaries were published in large number and in many languages in every country out of which several are known as international dictionaries.

(2) Size of Dictionaries

Dictionaries are published in many different sizes:

(a) **Abridged dictionaries** – At the starting point dictionaries were in small size which were having selected words. In modern period there are many dictionaries in small/abridged size which are being used in small libraries and schools and also in small business. For example: *New Century English Dictionary*, *Shorter Oxford English Dictionary*, *Bhargava English Dictionary*.

(b) **Enlarged dictionary** – All large libraries are having enlarged dictionaries as such they are useful to the researchers and students in their higher studies. Such dictionaries are *Webster's New International Dictionary*, *Oxford Advanced Learner's Dictionary*, *Frank and Wegnell New Standard English Dictionary*, *Hindi Menak Shabdkosh*, and *Hindi Shabd Sagar*.

(3) Types of Dictionaries

(a) **Glossary** – It is such dictionary in which idea introduction is mentioned. Glossary has its own importance. It includes technical words constructed with their explanations.

Example: ALA Glossary of Library Term.
A Consolidated Glossary of Technical Terms.

(b) **Lexicon** – Lexicons are used in the sense of dictionaries. It is most popular in Greek, Arabic and Hebrew. Foreign dictionaries are sometimes called Lexicons. In Egypt dictionaries are named as Lexicon.

(c) **Vocabulary** – It is related with collection words of specific subject, work and activities. It is less used but demanded at important point of discussion or writing the articles or books. It is limited to compilation of limited words in a specific field.

Vocabulary word is derived from Latin word vocabularium.

(d) **Concordance** – It is a collection of the words being used in religious books or the authors. Such words are used less and in special cases and for specific studies.

Example:

1. Oxford Concordance Bibliography (Oxford University).
2. Concordance of Principal Upanishads & Bhagwat Gita (Central Book Depot, Bombay).

(e) **Dictionary of synonyms** – When many words have collection of one meaning they are called synonyms. There are many words which are used for one meaning and generally all words have the same meaning.

There are many dictionaries of synonyms published:

(i) Webster's Dictionary of Synonyms.

(ii) A Dictionary of Synonyms and Autonyms, etc.

(f) **Dictionary of abbreviations** – Abbreviation means the shortest form representing a large word or name. Abbreviations are used in every subject, persons or institutions name and literature. Readers also make queries about abbreviations.

Example:

(i) *Current Abbreviations* (Wilson, London)

(ii) *Dictionary of Abbreviations and Symbols* (New York: Cowoard McCami).

(g) **Dictionary of usage** – There are few special dictionaries published in which all important words are used in many directions. It means a word has many usage. Such dictionaries direct the readers and writers to use the words in adequate use.

Example:

(i) *Dictionary of Modern English Usage* (New York: Oxford)

(ii) *A Dictionary of Modern American Usage* (New York: Oxford University).

(h) **Dictionary of slangs** – The collection of words which are not the formal words used in conversation but informally used in a society in local language conversations are called dictionary of slangs. These words are not pure language words. Such words are generally used in rural areas. These words represent the actual science civilization and culture of a region.

Example:

(i) *Dictionary of Slangs and Unconventional English*. London: Routledge.

(ii) *American Treasury of Slangs*. New York: (Corwell).

(i) **Dictionary of phrases** – Phrases are always included or used in any language. They are based on the ancient culture, social behaviour, and human mind. Phrases are also used in traditional language. It is the duty of the library to collect them and make available to the readers. Phrases are collected and published in the form of dictionaries known as Dictionary of Phrases.

Example:

(i) *Brower's Dictionary of Phrases and Fables* (Cassell, New York).

(ii) *Dictionary of Foreign Words and Phrases* (Thomas and Hudson).

(j) **Subject dictionaries** – There are many dictionaries which cover one subject or group of subjects, such dictionaries are called subject dictionaries.

Example:

(i) Dictionary of Technical terms

(ii) Dictionary of Philosophy

(iii) Dictionary of Physics

(iv) Dictionary of Political Science.

(4) Language Classification of Dictionaries

Dictionaries can be categorized on the basis of the languages:

(a) Language dictionary

(b) Bilingual dictionary

(c) Multilingual dictionary

Language dictionary covers the words, their meaning of one language *i.e.* 'Oxford English Dictionary', 'Chambers English Dictionary'. The other category is bilingual dictionary. In such dictionaries the meaning of one word is given in other language. It covers into language words *i.e.* 'Bhargava's English Hindi Dictionary', Dr. Kamle's 'English Hindi Dictionary'. Bilingual dictionaries are helpful to translation work or general study of meaning of word of one language into other language. There are other dictionaries which cover more than two languages. For example: *Webster's New International Dictionary* in which meaning of one word is given in seven languages like Italian, French, German, etc.

(5) Evaluation of Dictionaries

There are factors to be considered while evaluating a dictionary, such as:

(a) Authority
(b) Format
(c) Word treatment
(d) Vocabulary
(e) Special features

(a) **Authority** – The publication of dictionaries in large number has created a problem of evaluation as no standard pattern has been followed while preparing a dictionary. The quality of dictionary depend on the ability of the writer, compiler or editor. There are publishers which are specialized in the publication of dictionaries. Editorial Board has its own importance. They select a word, discuss it in all senses, analyse it grammatically and translate it or make its explanation in true sense in which it is used or to be used.

Example:

Publishers:

1. R.R. Bowker Co., New York.
2. Encyclopedia Britannica Inc., New York.
3. Hindi Sahitya Sammelan, Allahabad.
4. Bhargava & Co. Allahabad.
5. Reader's Digest Book Inc., New York.
6. Random House Inc., New York.
7. O & C Merriam Co., New York.
8. Macmillan, London.
9. Nagri Pracharni Sabha, Varanasi.
10. International Academy of Indian Culture, Nagpur.

(b) **Format** – Small dictionaries are generally in small size. There are few small dictionaries which are in large size and in more than one volume. No doubt the dictionary in one volume is more economical than more volumes and saves the time in consultation. One volume may be consulted at one time. But if one dictionary is more bulky then it will not be convenient to consult and transport. Dictionary should have durable binding as it is usually consulted. Dictionary should be arranged alphabetically.

(c) Treatment of words – Word arrangement is an important work which is a basic point of a dictionary. Modern words should be selected for dictionary. There are precautions to be taken which are as under:

(i) Necessary words should be explained with pictures.

(ii) Words should be well spelled.

(iii) Clarity in words.

(iv) Words should be used in society.

(v) Historical background.

(vi) Complex language should be avoided.

Word arrangement should include:

(i) Proper definition

(ii) Word-letters

(iii) Pronunciation

(iv) Proverbs

(v) Proper examples

(vi) Practical formation of words.

These factors make the dictionary of high standard.

(d) Vocabulary – While compiling a dictionary we should consider the following factors:

(i) How far words are traditional

(ii) Whether dictionary will be large or small

(iii) Whether words include proverbs, slangs and examples and these are mentioned separately.

There is no limit of large and small dictionary. It cannot be according to the number of words. A small dictionary may mention between 1 lakh and 3 lakh words while large dictionary may mention between 3 lakhs to 6 lakhs. Therefore, the words should have explanations, pictures, meanings, proverbs and all possible details like definitions.

(e) **Special Features** – Important dictionaries compile all informations like pictures, historical dates, statistics, and life sketches.

Example:

Random House Dictionary has included 64 pages of Atlas, guide for College and University, 55 pages Gazetteers, famous historical dates, etc.

(6) Oxford English Dictionary

Oxford, Clarendon Press, 1989, Edition 2.

Introduction

It is an authentic and reliable dictionary of English language. This dictionary provides historical information of words such as origin, history and meaning which is important for understanding meaning of word. This dictionary is very important for whole world. It is a general dictionary which is a collection of words used in language. It is known by many names such as Oxford Dictionary or New English Dictionary (NED) or Oxford English Dictionary or Murray's Dictionary, etc.

Authority

(a) This dictionary was for the first time published between 1883-1928 in 10 volumes. Its name was at that time "New English Dictionary on Historical Principles".

(b) In 1933 this dictionary was published in 12 volumes under the name of "Oxford English Language" after this its 4 more supplements were published.

(c) Its reprint was published in 1961, 1970 and in 1978.

(d) Its 2nd edition was published in 1989.

Scope

(a) Words from language and literature to words of science and technology are included.

(b) Development of English words is represented by 186 million citations.

(c) In this dictionary there are about 4 lakh entries.

(d) In it, about 42,000 new terms of science and technology, terminology are included.

(e) An effort has been made to explain the history of words used since 10th century.

(f) At the beginning of this dictionary, abbreviations, explanations and symbols used in it are given.

Treatment

In this dictionary following informations are given in entries of words:

(a) Spelling of words

(b) Pronunciation

(c) Definition

(d) Etymology, part of speech

(e) Syllabification

(f) Citation of author

Special Features

(a) Famous English words used from 1150 AD upto the present time are included.

(b) In this dictionary detailed meaning of each word is given.

(c) The trend is to include words that have come into English language from other languages (Chinese, Yiddish, Indian and others) due to foreign influence on the English language specially in USA.

(d) In it, along with the old meaning new meanings are also included.

(e) In the last volume complete bibliographical detail has been given.

Arrangement

(a) Arrangement of words is alphabetical.

(b) List of abbreviation also has alphabetical arrangement.

Physical Format

(a) Binding is of hardboard.

(b) Printing is clear and easy to read.

(c) Paper of good quality is used.

Merits

(a) It is standard dictionary of English language in which development of English is studied through historical sequence.

(b) To keep this dictionary uptodate, new words have been added and for this reason new editions are published from time to time.

(c) Oxford Dictionary is most complete, authentic, scholarly and famous dictionary of English language, based on historical principles.

(d) Historical record of development and changed meaning of words are given.

Demerits

(a) Though the words are taken from many sources and earliest records, yet many words are left out.

(b) Many libraries cannot purchase it as it is very costly but now it is available in small size with economical price. For studying small size dictionary magnifying glass is used.

Conclusion – Oxford dictionary is most important dictionary of English language. This dictionary is a useful reference source.

(7) Webster's Third New International Dictionary of the English Language

Introduction

Dictionary is a collection of terms of a subject or words of language. In dictionary definition, pronunciation, meaning, use, synonym, antonym of words are given. Symbols used for words, history, foreign vocabulary, idioms, illustrations, maps are also included.

Webster's Third New International Dictionary is an important dictionary of English language. This is an unabridged dictionary which comes under the category of general dictionary. In it, vocabulary of 7 languages have been included.

Authority

(a) Its publication has been done by Encyclopedia Britannica, Chicago.

(b) It is in 3 volumes.

(c) This latest unabridged Merrian Webster is 8th in the series which has its beginning in New Webster's American Dictionary of the English Language 1828.

(d) In making of this dictionary many editorial staff and outside consultants contributed as mentioned below:

Editor-in-Chief	1
Associate Editors	13
Assistant Editors	58
Additional Assistants	66
Secretarial and Clerical Assistants	31
Outside Consultants	200

Scope

(a) In this dictionary, 45 lakh new examples have been recorded. In it, more than 16,65,000 citations have been added.

(b) The dictionary has a vocabulary of about 45 lakh words. Vocabulary given in this dictionary is shown from pages 1-2662 under "A Dictionary of English Language".

(c) In this dictionary, explanatory notes, spellings, plurals capitalization, writing of compounds, Merriam Webster pronunciation symbols, division in bold faced entry words, guide to pronunciation, punctuation, abbreviations used in this dictionary, special symbols, etc. have been given.

(d) In the last of Volume III, important words are given in seven languages.

The Britannica world dictionary given in the last of Volume III is divided into two parts:

Part I: English to Other Language List

Part II: Other Language to English List.

Part I

(i) It begins from page 2681 of this volume, is a list of common English words, with their translation into six other languages – French, German, Italian, Spanish, Yiddish and Swedish.

(ii) Besides the word list proper, following special material is included in Part I – letters of the alphabet, cardinal numbers, ordinal numbers, days of week, months of the year and common first name.

Part II

(i) It begins on page 2777 of this volume, is an almost exact reverse of part I. It consists of 6 separate sections, an alphabetical word list for 6 other languages with the pronunciation of each word and English translation of each.

(ii) The same special list that appears in Part I (alphabets numbers, days of week, etc.) also appears in part II but is realphabetised according to the particular language.

(iii) Each of language section also contains a list of useful expressions and explanation of general grammar and key to pronunciation.

(e) In volume 3 of this dictionary, list of abbreviations, helpful hints for use of the Britannica world language dictionary are given.

Treatment

(a) This dictionary is of English language in which 6 other languages are included and arranged with their various symbols and vocabulary, *e.g.*

According – adj [ME, fr. Pres of accorden to accord] archaic: AGREEING, HARMONIOUS, < this voice of National Wisdom – Edmund Burke >

i.e. adj – adjective, ME – Middle English, fr – from
pres – present, president
part – participle

(b) Entries given in this dictionary are expressed in the form of explanatory chart. One or more part of each entry is given in margin box linked by an oval line with the entry.

(c) To explain entries easily, explanatory notes are given in which following informations are given:

The main entry, pronunciation, functional label, inflectional forms, capitalization, attributive noun, the etymology, phrases, the symbolic colon, synonyms, abbreviation symbols, the vocabulary entry, etc.

(d) The bold faced word used in it are explained in detail under 'Division in Bold face entry words'.

(e) To explain the words of all languages given in it, detailed spellings of words are given, *e.g.* derivatives, variants.

(f) List of abbreviations used in this dictionary is given along with the list of special symbols.

New words included in this are kept in Addenda Section.

Towards the end of Part I of *Britannica World Language Dictionary*, words of English language are given in other languages. For example:

English	French	German	Italian	Spanish	Swedish	Yiddish
a (an)	un, une	ein, eine	un, uno, una	un, una	en, ett	a, an

In Part II main words of language and Grammar are given as follows:

French Language
Main words (French special list)
Alphabet

a AH
b BAY

	French	Pronunciation	English
Cardinal Number	un, une	UHNGUN	One
Ordinal Number	sixieme	See – Z YEMM	Sixt

Useful expression – Following types of words are arranged–

Greetings, ordinary conversation, foreign language, asking directions, the hotel, the restaurant, telephoning, time, weather, postal information, barber and beauty shop, transportation, auto travel, public signs, etc.

Grammar – It includes grammar of all languages explained in easy way such as articles, nouns, pronouns, verbs, adjectives, etc.

Under basic key to pronunciation vowels and consonants are kept.

Special Features

(a) In this dictionary, words of 7 languages are arranged.

(b) Bold faced letter and symbols, light faced letters and symbols and italic words are used.

(c) Illustrations are also given in it as required.

(d) In this dictionary, grammar along with vocabulary of all 7 languages is taken.

(e) Pronunciation of the words of other languages is given in English language.

(f) In order to search the entries in it, directions are given as needed.

Arrangement

(a) Arrangement of words is alphabetical, word by word.

(b) Abbreviations used in this dictionary are also arranged alphabetically.

(c) Addenda section is also arranged alphabetically.

(d) Every part of English and other languages is arranged alphabetically.

Merits

(a) In order to make it up to date in the form of

supplementary "A supplement to Webster Volume III *New International Dictionary*" is published.

(b) It is a useful inference book for all types of libraries in which vocabulary of 7 languages is used at a place.

(c) Grammar of all languages is also shown in easy way in it. Each word is presented in this dictionary in easy form so that user can understand it and for this, various signs and abbreviations are used.

Demerits

(a) This dictionary is very costly so all libraries cannot buy it.

(b) Common users cannot understand it easily because various types of signs are used in it.

(c) It is difficult to understand the entries in it because seven languages are used in it.

Conclusion – This dictionary is very important for all type of libraries through which we can get the knowledge of vocabulary of seven languages and appropriate knowledge of grammar is also obtained.

(8) Important Dictionaries

1. *Websters New International Dictionary of English Language*. Springfield, Merriam, 1971.
2. *New Standard Dictionary of English Language*, New York: Funk & Waguller, 1950.
3. *Oxford English Dictionary*, Oxford: Clarendon Press, 1933.
4. *A Dictionary of American English on Historical Principles*. University of Chicago, 1936-44, 4 vols.
5. *Century Dictionary and Cyclopedia*, New York: Century, 1911.
6. *Random House Dictionary of English Language*. New York: Random House, 1966.
7. *Webster's New World Dictionary*. World Pub. Co., New York, 1965.

8. *Universal Dictionary of English Language*. London: Routledge, Kagan Paul, 1937.
9. *Dictionaire de l' Academic Francaise*. Paris: Hachette, 1931-35. 2 vols. (French).
10. *Nouvean Petit Laroussa Illustre Dictionaire Encyclopedique*, Paris: Larousse, 1960-64.
11. *Deutsches Worterbuch Leipziq Hirzel*, 1938. 16 vols. (German).
12. *Ilnovssimo Melzidionario Italiano* in due parti, Linguisrica Scientifica. Milan: Vallerdi, 1956. 2 vols. (Italian).
13. *Diccinario de la Langue Espanola*. Madrid: Espasa Calpof, 1938 (Spanish).
14. *Dictionary of Russian Language*. Moscow: Academy of Science (Russian).

Abridged Dictionaries

1. *New Century Dictionary of English Language*. New York: Appleton Century–Crafts, 1948. 2 vols.
2. *Shorter Oxford Dictionary on Historical Principles*. Oxford: Clarendon. 2 vols.
3. *American Collegiate Dictionary*. New York: Funk and Wagnells, 1947.
4. *Webster's New College Dictionary*. New York: Random House, 1950.
5. *New College Standard Dictionary*. New York: Funk and Wegnells, 1951.
6. *Macmillan Modern Dictionary*. New York: Macmillan, 1951.
7. *The Concise Oxford Dictionary of Current English*. Oxford: Clarendon Press, 1951.
8. *Cassell's New English Dictionary*, Cassell, 1950.
9. *Everyman's English Dictionary*. Dent: Everyman Library.
10. *Webster's Student Dictionary*. Cincinnati: American Book Co., 1945.

11. *Standard High School Dictionary*. New York: Funk and Wegnells, 1950.
12. *Dictionary for Young People*. Philadelphia: Winston, 1948.

(9) Multi-lingual Dictionaries

1. *English-French-German-Scrbecreation*. New York: Arthar Vanous.
2. *Dictionary of Urdu, Classic Hindi & English*. Oxford: University Press.

Dictionaries of Social Science & Humanities

1. *Dictionary of Social Science*. Washington: Public Affairs Press, 1961.
2. *A Dictionary of Statistical Terms*. London: Oliver.
3. *Dictionary of Modern Economics*. New York: Bernes & Noble.
4. *The Dictionary of International Affairs*. Washington: Public Press.
5. *Dictionary of Linguistics*. New York: Philosophical Libraries.
6. *Standard Dictionary on Folklore Mythology & Legend*. New York: Funk Wegnells.
7. *Dictionary of Education*. New York: Barnes & Noble.
8. *A Compound Dictionary of Psychological and Psychoanalysis Terms*. New York: Longman.
9. *The Dictionary of Religion and Ethics*. New York: Macmillan.
10. *New Dictionary on Psychology*. New York: Philosophical Library.
11. *Dictionary of Philosophy*. New York: Philosophical Library.

Dictionaries of Science

1. *Medical Dictionary*. London: Blackbell.
2. *Dictionary of Mathematical Sciences*. New York: Fredrick Ungler Pub.

3. *Dictionary of Anthropology*. London: Peterowen.
4. *Dictionary of Astronomy and Astronautics*. New York: Philosophical Library.
5. *Condensed Chemical Dictionary*. New York: Reinhold Pub. Corp.
6. *Van Nostrand Chemist's Dictionary*. New York: Princeton: N.I.D. Van Nostrand.
7. *Dictionary of Atomic Terminology*. New York: Philosophical Library.
8. *Dictionary of Physics & Electronics*. Princeton: N.I.D. Van Nostrand.
9. *Dictionary of Computer and Control System Abbreviations, Signs and Symbols*. New York: Odyssey.
10. *Elsevier's Dictionary of Nuclear Science and Technology*. Amsterdom: Elsevier Pub. Co.
11. *Dictionary of Mechanical Engineering*. New York: Philosophical Library.

(10) Indian Dictionaries

1. *Students' New Sanskrit Dictionary into English*. Marathi and Gujarati. Bombay: Keshava Bhikaji Dhovele, 1955.
2. *Swastic Dictionary* (English, Marathi, Gujarati), Rajahmundry: Swastik Book Depot, 1969.
3. *Isedi English-Hindi-Malyalam Nighantu*. Trivandrum: Educational Supplier Depot, 1968.
4. *Bharti Vyavaharik Kosh* (Hindi). Bombay, 1961.
5. *Dictionary of Urdu, Classical Hindi and English*. London: Oxford University Press, 1968.
6. *Regmi-Sanskrit Traibhashik Kosh* (Sanksrit, Nepali-Hindi-English) Varanasi, 1960.
7. *Shabd Bhasha Manjari*. Madras: Vavilla: Renaswami-Sastrulu, 1957.
8. *Arbachu Raj Vyavaharik Kosh* (English, Marathi, Hindi). Bombay: Sahitya Mandir, 1962 (Hindi).
9. *Student's Concise Modern Dictionary* (English, Marathi

and Gujarati). Bombay: Kesava Bhikaji Dhavale, 1958.

10. *Swan Oxford Packet Dictionary*. (Engish-Hindi-Punjabi) Jallandhar: Raj Pub., 1960.
11. *Govt. Karya Vyavhar Paribhasha* (English-Bengali-Hindi). Calcutta, Bengal Home Ministry, 1958.

(11) Subject Dictionaries

1. *Pustakalaya Gyan Kosh*. Patna: Rastra Bhasha Parishad, 1961 (Hindi).
2. *Glossary of Cataloguing Terms*. New Delhi: ISI, 1969.
3. *Kriya Kosh*. Calcutta: Jain Darshan Samiti, 1969 (Religious).
4. *Bhogolik Kosh*. Ahmedabad: Vernacular Society, 1935 (Hindi).
5. *Geographical Dictionary of Ancient and Medieval India*. New Delhi: Oriental, 1971.
6. *Itihas Sthanaval*. New Delhi: Ministry of Education, 1969.
7. *Vishwa Itihas Kosh*. Bhanpur: Gyan Mandir. 5 vols.
8. *Bhartiya Sanskrit Kosh*. Poona: Bhartiya Sanskrit Kosh Mandal, 1962.
9. *Vivid Shabd Sagar*. Agra: Wadhwa, 1951.
10. *Law Dictionary*. Lucknow: Eastern Book, 1970.
11. *Dictionary of Law Terms*. Patiala: Sardar Atma Singh, 1950.
12. *Rajkiya Kosh*. Allahabad: Central Book, 1948 (Hindi).
13. *Bhartiya Rajnitikosh*. Poona: Koolkaemi, 1948.
14. *Dictionary of Political Terminology*. Bombay: Jaico, 1971.
15. *Manovigyanic Paribhashit Shabd Kosh*. New Delhi: S. Chand, 1970.
16. *Angrezi-Hindi Vigyanic Kosh*. Allahabad: Bhartiya Hindi Parishad, 2 vols.

17. *Padmakosh*. Varanasi: Chowkhambha, 1951 New (Hindi).
18. *Prarambhik Kosh*. Vanaspati Vigyan. Delhi: Prakashan Vibhag, 1967 (Hindi).
19. *Terms in Botany: Invertebrates*. Travancore University, 1943.

Special Dictionaries

1. *Glossary of Phrases with Prepositions*. N.Delhi: Prentice Hall of India, 1965.
2. *English Idioms and How to Use Them*. Madras: Oxford, 1958.
3. *Hindi Muhavare*. Calcutta Vishwavidyalaya, 1969 (Hindi).
4. *Lokoktiyan and Muhavare*. Allahabad: Hindi Bhawan, 1933.
5. *Bundeli Kahavat Kosh*. U.P. Govt. (Hindi).
6. *Hindi Paryavachi Kosh*. Allahabad: Ram Narainlal (Hindi).
7. *Nirala Kavya Kosh*. Kurukshetra: Alok (Hindi).
8. *Prasad Kavya Kosh*. Varanasi: Hindi Pracharak Pustakalya.
9. *Dictionary of Indian Quotations*. Delhi: Bright Institute.
10. *Hindustan Kahawat Kosh*. New Delhi: National Book Trust, 1968.
11. *Glossary of Indian Logic*. Delhi: International Academy of Indian Culture.
12. *The Elements of Style*. New York: Macmillan.
13. *A Dictionary of Modern English Usage*. New York: Oxford University Press.

(H) GAZETTEER

A list of place names published as a book or at the end of a book is known as Gazetteer. It is official document published by a particular organization containing important information about decisions that have been made and people who have been employed.

According to *Encyclopedia Britannica* "Gazetteer is a list of cities, rivers, mountains, etc. which are arranged alphabetically." Index given in Atlas is also called Gazetteer because all geographical informations and necessary directions are given in it. But geographical dictionaries do not have maps and informations are given with details. There are other informations that also given like historical, commercial, Industrial, cultural and statistical informations.

Gazetteers have following specific features:

(a) Names of the cities are given.

(b) It has limitations, *i.e.* India Gazetteers.

(c) All information about places is given.

We can categorize Gazetteers as under:

(a) Independent Gazetteers
Example – *Chamber's World Gazetteers.*

(b) Index of Atlas
Example – Index to Andress Allgemeiner Hand of Atlas.

(c) Composit Gazetteers
Example: *Dictionaries and Atlas Combined Gazetteer.*

(1) Gazetteer of the Province of Oudh

Introduction

In Gazetteer, geographical information related to states, cities, rivers, mountains, population, places, etc. is given. In *Gazetteer of Oudh*, reliable information is given. The information given in it is useful for all types of users. In this geographical source, all informations related to Oudh Province from 1877-78 are given.

In British period, organization of province was different. Under Province of Oudh major part of U.P. and some parts of other states combined from Oudh and Agra Provinces were included. In this Gazetteer information of Oudh Province is given.

Authority

(a) Low Price Publication, Delhi brought the publication of this Gazetteer.

(b) The first edition was published in year 1877-78.

(c) Its reprint edition was published in 1993.

(d) It is three volumes in one:

- (i) Volume I A to G (with Index)
- (ii) Volume II H to M (with Index)
- (iii) Volume III N to Z (with Index)

(e) With a total area of 23,930 square miles, Oudh lies between the extreme latitudes of 25°34' and 29°6' and longitude of 79°45' and 83°11' east.

(f) To the east and the west it is enclosed by the older acquired districts of the North-West Provinces with Jaunpur, Basti and Azamgarh on one side and Shahjahanpur, Farukhabad and Cownpore on the other.

Scope

(a) In this Gazetteer the information of whole Oudh is given for example:

- (i) Rivers – Ganga, Tapti, Gomti, Gogra
- (ii) Jhils – Behti and Sandi
- (iii) Animal and Birds:
  1. Wild animals – Elephant, Buffalo, Tiger, Leopard, Pig, Black Buck, Duck, Peacock, Snake, Wolf.
  2. Domestic animals – Horse, Cow, Cattle, Donkey, Pig, Sheep, Goat, etc.
- (iv) Trees – Banian, Pipal, Shisham, Shakhu or Sal
- (v) Climate – The rains, the clouds, the hot weather.

  Chart of total rainfall from 1864-1874 is also given in it.
- (vi) Agriculture – f.1 – Crops – Kharif, Rabi

  f.2 – Vegetables – Potato, Carrot,

Onion, Garlic, Cabbage, Ghuiyan, Cucumber

(vii) History of Oudh

(viii) Religion.

(b) In this Gazetteer total 12 districts are covered:

Volume I – 4 districts
Volume II – 4 districts
Volume III – 4 districts

(c) About districts given in each volume, information is covered chapterwise as follows:

Chapter 1 – National Features
Chapter 2 – History
Chapter 3 – General Material, Social, Economical and Administrative Aspects.
Chapter 4 – Land Tenures
Chapter 5 – Agriculture, Trade and Commerce
Chapter 6 – The People.

Treatment

(a) In this Gazetteer each chapter is divided into Sections to arrange information as:

Chapter 1: Natural Features

Latitude, Longitude, Area, Position and boundaries, Physical Features, Rivers, Forests, Climate, Rainfall, Roads, etc.

Chapter 2: History

Section (i) – Mythic Period
Section (ii) – Buddhist Period
Section (iii) – Bhars Period
Section (iv) – Subsequent Muhammadan invasion and settlement
Section (v) – The districts in the thirteenth century
Section (vi) – The Muhammedan and Rajput settlement 1340 A.D. – 1450 A.D.
Section (vii) – The districts at the end of the fifteenth century

Section (viii) – Akbar 1556-1605 A.D.
Section (ix) – The Raikwars
Section (x) – The Janwars
Section (xi) – The Northrn Pargana
Section (xii) – The Southern Pargana during the Nawabi Rule.

Chapter 3: General Material, Social, Economical and Administrative Aspects

Administrative Division and Official Staff, Courts, Revenue, Expenditure, Police and Crime, Taxation, Education, Post Office, Medical Aspect, etc.

Chapter 4: Land Tenures

The owners and tenures of the soil, the tribal distribution, uneven distribution of property, tricidence of land revenue, extract from Settlement Report, property of the holders, transfer of property.

Chapter 5: Agriculture, Trade and Commerce

Agriculture, Harvests, General Agricultural Features, Irrigation, Ploughing & Animal Husbandry, Prices, Famine Prices, Wages, Weights & Measures, Markets, Manufactures, Trades, Communication, Railways, Carriage, etc.

Chapter 6: The People

Population of the district, occupation of the people, religion, castes, meaning of the castes.

Special Features

(a) Data is represented through charts and tables, as:
  (i) The revenue of district in 1871-72.
  (ii) Table of accidental deaths for the years 1867-72.
  (iii) Average fall of rain in Faizabad district.
  (iv) Crime statistics for Gonda District.

(b) According to need footnotes are also given, for example:
  (i) + Elliots Supplementary Glossary, Chandel and Gautam

(ii) * Volume III page 278, Berlin Edition

(iii) * See paragraph 332, Sultanpur Settlement Report.

Name of pargana, tehsil and district are given in capital letters for example:

AMOSI – Pargana
BIJNORE – Tehsil
LUCKNOW – District LUCKNOW

(d) Use of bold and italic letters is made, for example:

District Bahraich, area and population
(This title is given in italics in the Gazetteer)

Arrangement

(a) Names of all towns and districts are arranged alphabetically, for example:

Volume I A to G

AGAI – Pargana Rampur – Tehsil BIHAR – District PARTAPGARH AHANKARIPUR – Pargana AMSIN – Tahsil FAIZABAD – District – FAIZABAD BAHRAICH DISTRICT ARTICLE.

Volume II H to M

HAIDARABAD – Pargana – Tahsil NIGHASAN – District KHERI HARDOI DISTRICT ARTICLE.

Volume III N to Z

NABINAGAR – Pargana LAHARPUR – Tahsil – SITAPUR – District SITAPUR PRATAPGARH DISTRICT ARTICLE.

(b) In this Gazetteer to arrange towns and district alphabetically the first three alphabets are taken in capital from the spelling of each name of towns or districts for example:

AIG-AJO	AJGAON
	AJODHYA
ALD	ALDEMAU
BAH	BAHRAICH
FYZ	FYZABAD

(c) A separate index is given with each volume in which arrangement is alphabetical, for example:

Vol. I A to G (with Index)

Abdul Wahid, conquers Suhelpur 255

Abhai Chand, Raja, enters OUDH 364-65

Vol. II H to M (with Index)

Abdulla Beg, Chakladar, 66

Vol. III N to Z (with Index)

Accidental death, Partabgarh – 133, Raibareli – 215
Sitapur – 380, Sultanpur – 442, Unao – 539

Physical Format

(a) Binding consists of hardboard.

(b) Printing is clear and easy to read.

Merits

(a) In Gazetteer, almost whole of the information published in government Gazetteer is included.

(b) This Gazetteer is more useful for persons and researchers related to History and Geography.

(c) The information given in the Gazetteer is reliable.

(d) From this Gazetteer whole information of Oudh province can be obtained.

(e) Its speciality is that with its each volume index of that volume is given as a result of which reader does not face any problem in consulting and understanding this Gazetteer.

(f) This Gazetteer is a compact reference source in which historical, geographical, cultural and economic information is given.

(g) The arrangement of information in this Gazetteer is alphabetical due to which a layman can also understand this Gazetteer.

Demerits

(a) It is not a continuous publication.

(b) The information given in it is not up to date.

(c) The style of writing this Gazetteer makes it difficult to understand by common people.

(d) As yearbook is published from time to time the use of Gazetteer is limited to historical point of view.

(e) It lacks bibliography due to which study of any fact in detail becomes difficult.

(f) Some Gazetteers are not published regularly because they contain same information which is given in Government Gazette. But due to Government bureaucracy either its publication occurs after long interval or the Gazetteer lacks whole information.

Conclusion – It is an Indian Geographical source which is related to Oudh province giving all its important information. Therefore, this is an important reference source for all kinds of users.

(2) Imperial Gazetteer of India

It was published under the authority of His Majesty Secretary of State of India in Council Oxford, Clarendon Press, 1907-09 in 26 volumes.

It is an authentic reference book. It gives geographical details and historical background of India. Its first edition was published in 1881 in 9 volumes. The third edition was published in 1907-09 in 26 volumes. It was reprinted a few years back. In this Imperial Gazetteer entries are arranged alphabetically. This reference book includes the following informations:

(a) Contemporary history of India

(b) Geographical informations

(c) Agricultural informations

(d) Industrial informations

(e) Administrative informations.

(3) Important Gazetteers

1. *Chamber's Word Gazetteer and Geographical Dictionary*. Edinburgh: Chambers, 1954.

2. Columbia Lippincott. *Gazetteers of the World.* New York: Columbia University Press, 1962.
3. *Webster's Geographical Dictionary.* Mass: Marrium, 1959.
4. *Time Index Gazetteers of the World.* New York: Haughton Millin, 1965.
5. *The Wonder World of Land and Water.* Paris, 1966.
6. *Boundaries, Areas, Geographical Centres of the United States.* Washington: Govt. Ptg. Press.
7. *Survey Gazetteer of the British Isles.* Edinburgh: Bartholomew.
8. *Dictionnaire Geographique et Administratio de la France.* Paris: Hachette.

Indian Gazetteers

1. *Imperial Gazetteer of India.* Oxford: Clarendon Press. 26 vol.
2. *Maharashtra Gram Kosh* (Hindi). Poona: Maharashtra Gramkosh, 1967. 2 vol.
3. *Gazetteer of India.* Govt. of India, Ministry of Information and Broadcasting, Centre Gazetteer Unit.

(I) GUIDE BOOKS

According to ALA Glossary, guide books are such handbooks which are used by the travelers/tourists for their guidance. Guide books mention cities, places, countries and their historical places, buildings, museums and religious monuments.

Dr. Ranganathan has defined the guide books as small directories giving historical informations of a country. In addition to this, other informations like museums, art galleries, cultural buildings, natural places, transportation facilities to visit the places and distance of the cities and places, etc. are also given.

William A. Kunj has defined the aim of the guide book as to guide the travelers about the cities, places and historical buildings. There are other informations mentioned in the guide book:

(a) Car agencies

(b) Institutions

(c) Offices

(d) Roads and their situations.

Guide book is an important reference book. It guides not only the travelers but also the laymen giving informations about city bus service, trans service, metro services, city roads, location of educational institutions, etc. There are many types of guide books:

(a) Road Guides

(b) Tourists Guides

(c) Monument Guides

(d) Transportation Guides

(e) Air Service Guides.

Guide books mention road maps, bus numbers, and also necessary maps to guide the tourists and countrymen.

Important Guide Books

1. *American Guide Series*
2. *Encyclopedia of World Travel*
3. *Tourist guides of India*. Tourist Deptt. Govt. of India
4. *Fodor's Modern Guides*. London: Nov. 1953.

Index